a gu

employing youth and children's workers

a guide for churches

employing youth and children's workers

Paul Godfrey and
Nic Sheppard

CHURCH HOUSE
PUBLISHING

Church House Publishing
Church House
Great Smith Street
London SW1P 3AZ

Tel: 020 7898 1451
Fax: 020 7898 1449

ISBN 978 0 7151 4058 1

Published 2008 by Church House Publishing

Printed in England by Cromwell Press Ltd
Trowbridge, Wiltshire

Contents

Foreword

In recent years a growing number of churches have wanted to appoint a paid youth or children's worker – but haven't always known where to go for help and guidance. This publication will be invaluable in bridging the span between the initial thoughts of employing a worker to managing the person appointed.

As Diocesan Advisers of many years' experience, Nic and Paul have drawn on a variety of situations to help churches consider everything involved in making an appointment. Taking the principles of best practice, duty of care and good stewardship as their foundations, the authors have created a guide that helps churches think through what they are expecting from a paid appointment, offer guidance on how to plan for the appointment and give consideration to the ongoing management and development of the worker.

A very helpful section addresses the importance of job descriptions, contracts and managing the employment process. But care of employees does not stop with appointment, so there is also advice on management, supervision and ongoing training. While not claiming to give legal advice, the book points churches to the appropriate areas of employment law that will need to be considered.

This clear, accessible and, above all, practical guide is a welcome addition to the Sure Foundations series and we warmly commend it to any church considering the possibility of employing a youth or children's worker.

Peter Ball
National Youth Adviser for the Church of England

Mary Hawes
National Children's Adviser for the Church of England

Tribute to Paul Godfrey

Paul Godfrey, who died suddenly on 4 August 2007, aged only 50, was zealous for good children's work in Christian churches. This enthusiasm for children and the gospel came across in every aspect of his work and life.

Paul was Children's Adviser for the Diocese of Chelmsford for six years. During his time there, he helped develop a clear strategy for churches to reach out and to nurture children through a wide range of ideas and activities. He had also worked to ensure coordination between children's and youth work and work with families as a whole. He had supported, mentored, encouraged and cajoled church leaders at all levels to seek the highest possible standards.

His concern to ensure that those who worked with children and young people were adequately supported led him to develop 'best practice' guidelines for the diocese on recruiting and employing children's workers – work on which this book is partly based.

Paul believed that Jesus meant it when he said 'of such is the kingdom of heaven'. Alongside his diocesan work, he played a key part in children's work nationally. He was a highly valued member of the children's advisers team, offering crucial support to the national advisers and supporting his colleagues throughout the network.

Prior to his work in Chelmsford, Paul was a Scripture Union children's evangelist and before that a modern languages teacher. He was also a Reader in the Church of England and fully involved in the life of Christ Church, Bedford.

Paul was married to Caroline and she and their three children, Hannah, Andrew and Richard, meant more to him than anything else.

Paul was a thinker and inspirer of others who held his love of children alongside his Christian faith. He was a role model for children's work and influenced many in the Church of England and in wider national and European networks.

I was privileged to know him as one of his Southampton teachers, as well as being his team leader in Chelmsford Diocese. He is greatly missed and I hope that this book will be seen as a fitting tribute to him.

Revd Canon Peter Hartley

Diocesan Director of Education, Diocese of Chelmsford

(with thanks to Bishop Paul Butler and the *Church Times* for extracts from the obituary that appeared in the *Church Times*, 28 September 2007)

Acknowledgements

Many thanks to those who contributed and helped in the production of this book, in particular to Sally Sheppard, Caroline Godfrey, Richard Burge, Liz Morton, Ben Mizen, Nicki Sudworth, Craig Groocock, Neal Terry, Chris Brewster, Tracey Messenger, members of the Church of England Youth Work and Children's Work Advisers network, Peter Ball, Yvonne Criddle and Mary Hawes (Church of England National Youth and Children's Officers), Diana Murrie (former Church of England National Children's Officer), the National Council for Voluntary Youth Services and Ecclesiastical Insurance Group. The list of standards in Appendix 4 is reproduced by kind permission of the National Council for Voluntary Youth Services, from their publication *Keeping it Safe*.

And finally, our thanks go to those many churches, projects, organizations, clergy and ministers, paid workers and volunteers upon whom our experience is based – both good and bad.

Introduction:
The importance of building on rock

This book is offered as a good practice guide for churches who are considering employing a paid children's, youth or family worker.

There have been a growing number of such appointments in the churches in recent years as churches seek to respond to issues such as:

- declining or static church attendance figures among young people (or conversely, a growing number of children and young people);
- a perceived widening of the gap between the young and the old;
- the apparent irrelevance of traditional church life for many families and young people.

Before rushing in to appointing a worker to respond to these perceived needs, it is worth taking time and care to research what kind of worker you need to employ and to make sure the whole process is done well. This book takes you through this process and will enable you to ensure that your future work with children, young people and families, including any possible paid appointment, is built upon rock and not on sand.

This book has been written by two diocesan advisers in the Church of England, one focused on work with children, the other with young people. Over the years, we have had a great deal of experience of advising churches who are considering or in the process of appointing a children's, youth or family worker. Diocesan and other denominational advisers are usually only too happy to help in such situations, and we recommend that you involve them from the outset.

All too often, however, we have been called in to help when an appointment has gone wrong, as in the following example:

St Knowall's had a thriving junior church, youth group and young mums group. With an existing mission budget of over £20,000 it seemed relatively easy for the church council to appoint a worker to lead these groups, and possibly take on the emerging schools work. A neighbouring church already had a youth worker so it was easy to obtain the necessary paperwork and make a few changes. The church warden's niece had just qualified as a youth worker and wanted to move back to the area so it was thought that by employing her money could be saved on advertising (and salary). Sadly, within six months tensions arose resulting in a dwindling number of Junior Church volunteers. The church council felt let down when the worker felt 'called' to move away and work for the neighbouring church.

This example, like all the case studies in this book, is drawn from real life (although names and details have been changed). A bit more care and planning will help you to avoid such an outcome, which may be disastrous for the church, its work with children and young people and for the employee. This book aims to help you avoid such mistakes, which are costly for all involved.

The church has a moral imperative to ensure that its work with children, young people and families is well researched, well resourced and undertaken with care.

Three principles: 'best practice', 'duty of care' and 'value for money'

These three principles are all terms commonly used in the management of local authority and commercial service delivery. The world now routinely sets regulations by which work and outcomes can be measured to ensure consistency and high standards.

When the Church seeks to set standards, the first place to start is to look to the model of Jesus himself, in the Gospels. From Christ's teaching to his disciples, today's church can draw many examples of best practice, duty of care and value for money, or *good stewardship*, as it is more commonly known in church circles.

Let's look at three examples from the teaching of Jesus.

1. 'Best practice' and the Good Samaritan

Jesus' parable of the Good Samaritan (Luke 10.25-37) offers us several aspects of best practice. For example:

- Appropriate response to need: the man is given the help and care he needs.
- Anti-discriminatory practice: a Samaritan breaks the norm in attending to his enemy.
- Generosity and self-giving: the Samaritan goes the extra mile and so much more.
- Proper follow-up: he checks his work has been, and continues to be, effective.

These four aspects are all particularly relevant in the planning and management of new work.

2. 'Duty of care' and the Good Shepherd

An analogy of a shepherd looking after his sheep recurs in St John's Gospel. In chapter 10 Jesus describes the high level of attention and commitment offered by the Good Shepherd who had taken on the duty of care for the sheep. In the final chapter Jesus commissions his followers to continue to care for his 'sheep'. In employing a paid worker or using volunteers, there is a duty of care on the part of both the workers and the 'employers'. Therefore, proper consideration has to be given to the necessary safeguards and support that need to be put in place to fulfil a duty of care.

3. 'Good stewardship' and the parable of the Talents

Many of the parables of Jesus refer to the principle of good stewardship. In his story of the servants entrusted with varying amounts of money (Luke 19.11 onwards) we can see the need to value and use resources wisely, rather than simply seek to store them away. When embarking on a new piece of work, it is further the responsibility of Christ's disciples to consider the long- and short-term requirements so that financial, human and practical resources are not too quickly exhausted or squandered.

Putting principles into practice

Even to consider employing a worker is a major step. It is essential that:

- the reasons for taking that step are prayerfully shared and understood;
- there is a clear vision and consensus over the way forward;
- high standards are set and maintained.

This book is intended to help with the process of exploring and sharing the vision and developing the practicalities of making it happen, and keeping it going.

If, after following the guidelines in this book, you don't make an appointment, it could be because you've identified a better way forward. If the book helps you make a good appointment, or at very least not make a poor one, it has done its job.

How to use this book

It is recommended that this book is worked through by the church committee or planning group who are considering whether employing a paid worker is the right step for the church. Where questions are included, take time as a group to work through them before moving on to the next stage.

Part One, Understanding the process, introduces the questions you need to consider right at the outset of the process and covers some essential definitions.

Part Two, Preparation process, is a step-by-step guide to the process itself, with questions for your church committee or planning group to work through. It covers research, planning, resourcing the work and identifying the tasks to be undertaken. This part should help you decide whether appointing a paid worker is the right step for you. If you do decide to go ahead, then you'll need to move on to Part Three.

Part Three, Appointment procedures, includes some background information on job descriptions and contracts and a guide to the recruitment process.

Part Four, Management issues, covers good management practice once a worker is in place.

The **Appendices** include a summary of all the questions in the book and sources of further help and advice.

An important cautionary note

While this book recommends a best practice model for considering the employment of a paid worker and gives advice on a recruitment process, it should not be considered as providing legal advice. At all points during the process, it is essential that churches seek appropriate advice from denominational advisers and from those with legal and human resources expertise.

Part One

Understanding the process

1 Laying firm foundations

Introducing a development process

There are a host of reasons why your church might be considering appointing a paid children's, youth or family worker. For example:

- You want to maintain your existing work with young people.
- Action needs to be taken to attract a missing generation.
- You want to nurture and keep the young people in your church.
- You want to attract new children, young people and families to the church.
- You recognize a particular community issue that you need help in addressing.
- You want to ensure that the gospel is effectively presented to this generation.
- You need some ongoing and on-the-spot 'expert' guidance.
- There's no one else to do the work.

For some churches, there may be other motives and underlying issues which, if left unchallenged, can result in problems for any appointment made. It is worth considering these from the outset.

For example, some churches employ a full-time worker to ensure the children or young people are usefully occupied away from the adults in the congregation who can then concentrate on the 'proper work and worship'. For such a church, the appointment of a worker may be the start of some real and unwanted challenges. Often when a worker is employed, transformations take place among the young people. As they become empowered, in the eyes of the adults in the church, they begin asking the wrong questions to the wrong people at the wrong time! This can be uncomfortable for all concerned and the worker may feel that they are held responsible. Many workers often feel that they are in a position where the people they are working for, and those they are working with, are at complete odds. This leaves them feeling unable to serve either group adequately, and consequently they become quite isolated.

To take another example, some churches have a sense of guilt that their income is primarily spent on maintenance. Employing a worker to begin a piece of work with children, young people and families can be a very visible way of spending the money proactively. However, this may well lead to a worker not having a clear remit as to the desired outcomes for the work. Also, problems may arise when maintenance becomes a priority and the worker may feel they are a drain on much-needed resources or even find they are redundant as a result.

So before you go any further, it is vital to consider the following questions:

- What has our church learnt from previous experience of developing work with a particular age group?
- What are our declared and undeclared reasons for focusing on this particular piece of work?
- How ready are we to face the challenges that new work will present?
- Are we committed to being patient and thorough?
- Who is prepared to take a lead in this development?

This book cannot answer the questions for you, as every situation will be different, but we hope that it will help you carefully and prayerfully to think through the issues. If there is enough commitment within the church to continue with the process, then you may move on to the next stage.

A 'best practice' process

Working through the process recommended in this book will help you to consider:

- What is this church's vision for work and ministry with children, young people or families?
- Who is the church particularly seeking to serve?
- What exactly would the church want a paid worker to do?
- What finances and resources are available?
- What management and support would be needed?
- How will the success of the work be measured?

Even if the appointment of a paid worker is appropriate, the work will still require the input and support of volunteers and therefore, at every stage, consideration is given to the effect a paid appointment will have on any existing unpaid workers.

The recommended process is in three distinct stages:

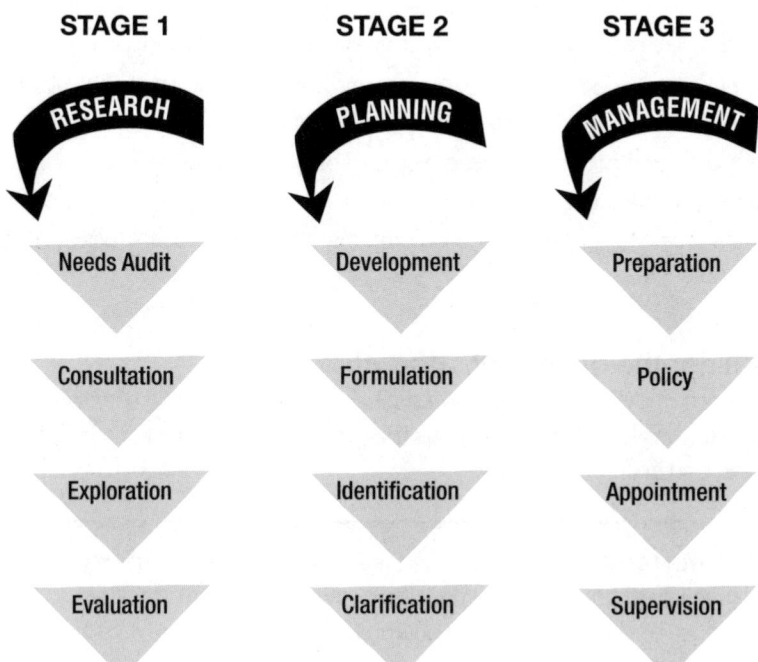

STAGE 1	STAGE 2	STAGE 3
RESEARCH	PLANNING	MANAGEMENT
Needs Audit	Development	Preparation
Consultation	Formulation	Policy
Exploration	Identification	Appointment
Evaluation	Clarification	Supervision

The process timescale

The enthusiast could be forgiven for thinking that this process could take just a few weeks to complete. In reality, it probably should take up to two years. Later chapters explore what each of the above components involves and the benefits of undertaking them. Time is needed not only to ensure the process is thorough, but also to allow space for prayer and reflection, and to test the resolve of those committing themselves to such an important undertaking.

Who should be involved?

Creating the right foundation involves a wide range of people, whose early input can significantly change the nature and direction of the project. While the list of those you might wish to talk to depends on your area and the proposed direction of your ministry, it would usually include:

- clergy and ministers both from your own and neighbouring churches;

- church/voluntary service advisers, such as regional and national children's and youth work advisers within the church and local authority;

- neighbourhood schools, clubs, organizations and professionals already actively involved with young people in your area;

- the church council, congregation and others, such as funders, who have a stake in the outcome;

- parents, young people and children that the project seeks to involve and serve,

Warning: the danger of short cuts

Experience shows that taking short cuts invariably lessens the effectiveness of both the work and the workers as the project is likely to lack clarity, broad support and secure resources.

St Well Meaning was challenged recently when a longstanding member of the congregation passed away bequeathing many thousands of pounds to the church for its work with the young people of the parish. Within six months a paid worker was in place, full of enthusiasm and vision. Six months later the worker had resigned citing their reasons as, 'Uncertain and conflicting goals, insufficient resources, poor management and supervision and the expectation to work unrealistic hours without proper assistance.'

The process that this book is advocating may result in the employment of a worker or workers. It may equally result in the decision not to *employ* a worker but to develop the work with children, young people and families in another way. While this outcome may appear less tangible, the effect of following the process itself can be just as significant.

- Many new relationships will be fostered.
- The church will grow in its understanding of and response to the community.
- Children, young people and families will benefit from being the focus of the church's prayer and attention.

2 Surveying the site

Clarifying essential terminology and definitions

Understanding these definitions, and the potential confusions around them, will help you develop your work and make decisions about appointing a paid worker.

Some existing definitions

Policy documents can bring confusion to *definitions* of terms such as 'child', 'youth', 'young adult'. For example:

- In education those who were previously described as 'children' or 'pupils' have now become 'young people' or 'students'.

- The government report *Every Child Matters* defines children as those aged up to 18, except if they are in care, in which case it's 19.

- Local authority Early Years Partnerships had been covering 0–18s.

- The Childcare Bill introduced in 2005 uses the term 'later years' to mean 5–7s.

- OFSTED Early Years deals with childcare registration for 0–7s.

Confused? You have every reason to be. This discrepancy in definitions means that it is not easy to find a generic title for the kind of post this book is dealing with. Many churches also use the term 'youth work' to cover a multitude of meanings. For some it is work with teenagers only. For others, 'youth work' might include all children and young people up to the age of 18, or even 25. Meanwhile, the common currency among children and young people in education is more likely to be based on school year groups.

How much does this matter? It is crucial. Unless there is a clear understanding of the target group for a specific piece of work, the worker, the employer and the children and young people themselves are likely to be confused and ultimately disappointed. It is important to recognize that the skills needed to work with different ages and the varying issues that they might bring are very different; workers with different age groups require different skills, knowledge and expertise. These must be considered and clarified prior to any advertisement for a new post.

'Youth worker' tends to be the default term used when a church considers employing someone to do something with the younger generation. It is a short, handy term, used in both secular and church circles, which sits easily as a description of a volunteer or an employed post holder. It is somehow more appealing than whatever term tends to be used for those working with children. The shadow of the Sunday School, with its 'superintendents' and 'teachers', is long, and rarely welcomed now.

So what other definitions do we need to clarify?

The issue is not just about age groups, although this is often the most obvious criterion with which to define a new piece of work. 'Family worker' is also appearing in job adverts, but often without a thought-through definition of family to go with it. For example, a worker needs to be clear about whether their role is to work with parents, with young children, or whether their remit is to develop work and worship that involves all ages. In a desire to retain flexibility and spontaneity, the role can appear so great that it either becomes overwhelming or loses any focus.

Titles such as minister, pastor and worker relate chiefly to the nature of the task, but they also reflect the church's respect and recognition for the role. They are all potentially ministry posts. This is the most important thing they all have in common. However, the tasks and the expected outcomes of the roles may be distinctive and need definition at the outset. The youth worker may feel that their remit adequately justifies them sitting with the young people on the wall or in the bus shelter for many hours. They will see the fruits of this as being relationship building and taking the Christian presence into the community. The adults in the church, whose vision was to employ a youth pastor, could hold very different expectations and will only see the worker's worth when the young people are actively involved in the life of the church. The same distinctions also need to be considered and clarified in relation to work with children. This can span the broad spectrum of Junior Church, schools work, after school activities, holiday clubs and play schemes.

What distinctions are important for all of these types of post?

None of these posts will be able to provide a replacement for a whole group of volunteers, unless you find someone who can not only multi-task, but be in multiple locations at the same time. Typically there are a number of activities happening in the limited time slots available in evenings and weekends. This is particularly important if you are considering a post to be shared across a number of congregations. So this leads to the first major distinction you will need to determine:

- Will the main task be to work directly with the target group?

  or

- Will the main task be to manage, coordinate and resource the (predominantly volunteer) teams who work with the children, young people or families?

It needs to be said at this very early stage that unless you have a very clearly focused need for someone to fill a certain gap in your provision and/or you have a well-established set of roles already, you will be best advised to set up a post of the second kind. A managing and resourcing role will make the best use of the volunteers, rather than seeking to replace them. Once you have someone on the staff, especially for the first time, they will be looked to by the clergy and volunteers for that kind of leadership. If you haven't looked for those abilities in your recruiting, and if the post holder is either unable or unwilling to take on that role, you may have a clash of purpose in the making.

What might you expect in each distinctive role?

Direct working	Coordinating
Skills with specific group(s) – *key*	Age-specific knowledge – *less important*
Tactical decision making – *short term*	Strategic planning – *long term*
Relating to the client group	Relating to a team
Planning and carrying out own work	Enabling others
	Training and management skills

Many posts will be a mixture of the two roles. However, it is important to identify which is the primary task and should take priority. The more diverse the job in terms of its direct working and coordinating focus, and of its age-group focus, the more skills and experience will be required of your worker. As a result, you will certainly have fewer qualified and experienced applicants to choose from.

Qualities and skills to consider

It is beyond the scope of this book to attempt to define tightly the qualities required in every possible kind of post, but the following need consideration:

1. **The balance of skills, knowledge, attitudes and values of the worker.** Any post will require a mix of these. Skills and knowledge can be clearly defined and are easily evidenced. The attitudes and values of potential workers also need to be explored. It is tempting to make assumptions about the kind of people who are likely to apply, but this often happens and can lead to problems. For example, while you may see the importance of engaging with the young people who gather on the church wall for a smoke, your future worker may be an anti-smoker who takes a no tolerance approach to the 'deadly weed', leading to possible conflict not only between worker and young people but also between worker and project. Many posts come to grief – and sadly many more young lives have been damaged inside the church and out – because of attitudes and values.

2. **Relationships, integrity and spiritual vitality are core values in all ministries.** In its work with children, young people and families the church has often placed more emphasis on the more visible assets of, say, energy and the ability to play a guitar or juggle. We can be tempted to think of work with the younger age groups as child-minding or entertainment rather than ministry. A proper understanding of faith and spiritual development will remind us that these core values are as important in the crèche or at the bus shelter as in the main body of the congregation.

3. **The needs of the target group that is to be worked with.** Not many people will have the gifts and skills to work with a very wide range of ages and issues, so be clear about what is needed. If you have a group

of ten-year-old girls who like handicrafts, don't employ a rugby coach. However, don't assume a rugby coach can't do craft work. Stereotypes can be unhelpfully limiting.

These are some of the basics, but you don't have to remember all this at once. This book is designed to help you work through and answer these and other relevant questions as you go along. So the next chapter will set you off at the beginning of the preparation process – the sensible place to start.

Part Two

Preparation process

3 Stage 1: The research

Introducing a suggested process of research to use when embarking on new projects or developing existing work

Too many projects and pieces of work fall flat because the 'house was built upon sand'. Using our knowledge of what has worked well in other places, here are some simple guidelines to help you in thinking about the first steps. What works well in one place may not be appropriate in another. The experiences of others, however, can often help inform and broaden our thinking. A key message of this book is that churches need to take sufficient time and care to build secure foundations for the development of work. This should take place well in advance of making available any paid appointment, if that is, in fact, the direction your church decides it should take.

The three stages set out in Chapter 1, 'Research', 'Planning', and 'Management' outline a simple, yet thorough, process of preparation that can save considerable time and cost and can bring many future benefits to the work and ministry of the church.

The first stage is research, which has four parts, as shown in the diagram below. This is a major task in itself and may require the church council to appoint a small team of people dedicated to researching the needs of the church and/or local community. We have included an example of a research questionnaire for such a Needs Survey in Appendix 3 at the back of the book. A suggested remit for such a group is set out at the back of the book. Some churches and projects have benefited from a small grant to employ a researcher or student to take the lead in collecting and collating the material. Even so, members of the congregation will need to be involved.

RESEARCH

CONSULTATION ▸ Exploration ▸ Assessment ▸ Evaluation

Consultation

It may sound like stating the obvious but it is crucial to identify exactly what it is that children, young people or their families in your area actually need, and what might help meet that need. For example, there is little to be gained from starting a football club to keep young people off the street if the local leisure centre with the right facilities provides the same every night of the week for free. Equally, just because the church warden's son or daughter needs a particular activity doesn't particularly mean anyone else wants it. People are pretty good at believing that what they want is what everyone wants. Equally, folk are quick to vote with their feet if what is being offered is not what they want or need.

A simple proforma to target specific groups enquiring, 'What can the church offer you?', with a few suggestions to get the thinking started, may be enough to capture a pretty realistic snapshot of current needs and wants.

A Mums and Tots Group may be the last thing that Ms Jones wants. Her own two-year-old makes enough noise without sitting with half a dozen others. What may be more appreciated is a second-hand clothing club to help make ends meet.

Make a start with just a few members of the church. Having looked at their answers, you may need to add or amend questions before embarking on anything wider, to gain the most useful information. An example can be found at the back of the book in Appendix 3. It may be feasible and considered useful to undertake something more thorough. Useful guidance on designing such surveys and questionnaires is readily available on the Internet.

Within congregations are members who through family, employment, neighbourhood, community projects, uniformed organizations and schools already have significant relationships in the area. A simple audit of church members could reveal a wealth of knowledge and experience that it would be wise to use. They will have valuable ideas and information both about the needs of these groups, and ways in which the church might appropriately respond.

If a particular age group becomes apparent, or already is the focus for development, then it may be necessary and appropriate to further consult that group and those already working with them specifically.

It may also be helpful to consult directly with other agencies and organizations in the area that are already offering services. The list might include:

- police
- schools
- local authority
- residents associations
- other local community groups
- neighbouring places of worship

All have an interest in supporting community initiatives. They will be able to provide current information and possibly useful recent research. Such organizations tend to be inundated with surveys and questionnaires and are therefore less likely to respond. Face-to-face meetings are preferable as this establishes what hopefully will become a positive relationship with the work, which may develop into ongoing support.

Ask everyone if there is someone else they think it would be useful to consult with. The wider the consultation, the better and more accurate the picture obtained, and the more chance there is of avoiding duplication, competition and even offence!

While this is a lot of work, it will not be wasted time.

St Desperate in the course of their audit made contact with the secretary of the Working Men's Club. When the church hall flooded, the WMC happily stepped in at the last minute offering an alternative venue for the children's holiday activities.

The fact that the church is asking others about the needs of the community can send out important messages that the church both cares and values the involvement of others. Often church members can see employment of workers as being a way of 'getting' people in, whereas the church's work should be about 'giving' service to the community.

A neighbouring church may be struggling with many of the same issues as you. Consulting them may reveal some common concerns and might open up all sorts of new possibilities of working together or complementing provisions in the community.

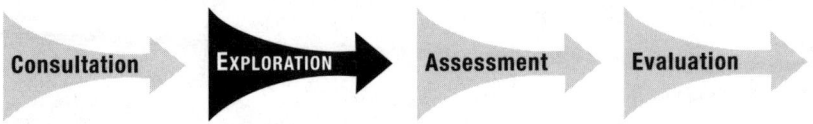

Consultation   EXPLORATION   Assessment   Evaluation

Exploration

This part of the research stage is about exploring what resources are already available. Take a look at the potential of your church buildings with an open mind as to the way in which they may be used. A common problem is that the property becomes more important than the work, or that the work does not take into account the limitations of the property. No point in starting up a playgroup if the polished floor will spoil as soon as paint gets spilt on it, or if the only room available has neither heating nor easy access to toilet facilities. So explore what is possible or what would be needed in order to adapt existing buildings and facilities.

Explore beyond your own surroundings. The Scout hut next door may be underused and the perfect setting for a new initiative if only your church was on speaking terms with the Scouts! Remember you don't have to do things on your own. Increasingly, funding is specifically available for work that is done in partnership. This may be with another church, voluntary organization or the local authority. The additional money to undertake new work with families, children and young people is often out there, even if you don't yet know how to get it. So find out what might be available and who might help you get it, but don't at this point commit to carrying out a piece of work simply to obtain the available funding. You should still be assessing need and exploring a variety of options.

'He, who pays the piper, calls the tune' does have particular relevance to any paid work. How the post or project is funded will reflect or even shape the nature and longevity of the work. Outside funders and local givers are keen to see that their money is spent on delivering particular outcomes. Fine, if this agenda meets the needs of those you are seeking to serve, the hopes of the managing group, the expectations of the sponsoring church. Not so good, if the availability of the money was the major motivating factor in taking on the work without first properly exploring and identifying the need, the support and the resources to deliver the goods.

St Sidelines discovered that the local authority was willing to grant substantial funding for a project that reduced juvenile crime on the local estate. Such was the urgency of the situation that little time was given to preparation. The management of the budget and supervision of volunteers both fell to the willing curate. Unfortunately, when the curate moved on a year later, the project could no longer be sustained. This led to disappointment and disillusionment for all concerned and jeopardized any future partnerships that the church might hope to enter into.

Assessment

This part of the research stage will help identify critical friends. Start by assessing the level of support available within your church for any new piece of work. Some people may have only just got used to the church council's last good idea. Once you have established a degree of support on the home front, and remembering it will never be unanimous, assess what outside help is available. Advice and support for a church and community initiative can come from a wide range of people. This could include officers from the wider church network, the local Council for Voluntary Services and other community work support groups. Using the assistance of an outside adviser or consultant at the various stages in planning and development can have clear benefits.

An adviser can offer initial and ongoing support in:

- determining and reviewing aims and objectives;
- creating the appropriate legal framework for a project;
- estimating costs and identifying sources of funding;
- sharing the experience and support of other projects and agencies.

And later, if a worker is to be employed, an adviser can assist in:

- establishing the terms and conditions of employment;
- advising on the advertising and appointment process;
- agreeing the means of induction, supervision and support for the post holder;
- drawing up working policies and procedures that ensure good and safe practice.

Not least, the adviser can both ask the questions others are avoiding and affirm a group who are beginning to wonder if they weren't just a little bit crazy to ever have considered such a bizarre idea.

Evaluation

The final part of the research stage is evaluating the potential costs and benefits. This will prove invaluable in deciding the course of action to be taken. There may be evidence of great potential benefits. There will be implications for staffing, funding, facilities, and so on. One aspect that is often overlooked is the impact new projects have on existing work.

> St Regenerate's study group for men always met in the church hall on Friday evenings. When asked to move elsewhere to make room for the new youth club, the members quite understandably felt sidelined and, as a result, were less than willing to offer valuable and much-needed support.

Whoever carries out the research stage, whether it's done entirely by members of the congregation or with the help of someone brought in specifically for the purpose, the findings will need to be presented to the decision-making bodies of the church. Having a summary of the findings with some suggested action ideas for further exploration, possibly accompanied by outline timescales and costings, will help the church decide how best to move into the next part of the process, the planning stage.

To think about . . .

- Given our location and the nature of the work, how extensive will our research need to be?
- What period of time may we need to allocate to the research stage?
- Who might we ask to oversee the research stage?
- Are there others outside the congregation whom it would be important to include at this early stage?
- How, where, and to whom, should the research be presented?

4 Stage 2: The planning

Why advance planning is crucial to a successful piece of work and suggested ways in which this could be undertaken

Following the completion of the research stage the church will be much better informed and equipped to move on to the planning stage.

Churches may not want to be a part of the world of audits, aims and objectives, strategies and the like. Yet every church operates with all of these to some degree, even if they are undeclared or couched in a different terminology. For example:

● The church leaders will most likely believe in their vision for the church community.

● The couple who lead the youth group may make prayerful plans and strategies for the next term's work.

● The church member who keeps an eye on the colouring books at the back of church and restocks when necessary is, in her own way, completing an audit and responding to the need.

Such diversity of service and delivery is one of the strengths of the church family. This diversity, for all its benefits, can result in some unnecessary negative tensions.

Many of the obstacles facing youth, children's and family workers developing their particular piece of work centre around others in the church believing in different approaches and priorities. Take a look at the following example.

Mr Green at St Action wants a campaign of door-to-door outreach to single parents on the local housing estate, encouraging them to come to family services. Ms Brown, herself a single parent, feels the church would be much better working together to set up a credit union. Although the two approaches could have worked side by side, the limited resources of the congregation meant a choice of which should come first had to be made.

Conflicting priorities can quickly disable a major piece of work, which makes it of utmost importance that there are agreed aims and objectives at the very beginning. The church's ministry can only benefit, and much more may be achieved, from taking time carefully and prayerfully to consider an agreed vision and develop a clear strategy. Tensions arise when purpose and responsibility are not understood or agreed.

Agreeing the vision or aim might be the relatively easy part. Here's one St Careful's 'prepared earlier':

> This church particularly seeks to reflect Christ's love for the young through its ministry, nurture and service to children, young people and their families.

Few in any church are likely to take exception to this. How this aim is actually to be achieved could offer as many methods as there are members in the church, plus a few others from outside. The possibilities are endless and therefore a process is required to help determine what the next steps should be and what resources are required.

A small appointed planning group may be well placed to help focus and steer the next stage of the process. There is a suggested remit for such a group in Appendix 2 at the back of the book.

PLANNING

DEVELOPMENT ➤ **FORMULATION** ➤ **IDENTIFICATION** ➤ **CLARIFICATION** ➤

The planning group
The purpose of the planning group is to develop and define a clear response to the findings of the earlier research work. They may have to sift through many possibilities, understand the implications, inform and make suggestions that help the church in choosing its direction. Whether developing existing work or undertaking a completely new project, there are substantial benefits in having such a group to review options, oversee, develop and bring focus

to the work. This applies whether the work is to be done by paid workers or purely by volunteers. The group may need to be properly representative of the church council and should include those with a particular interest in children's, youth and/or family work. Others from the wider community identified during the research stage may usefully assist by acting in an advisory role to the group. Members of this group may become the core of a future management group once the work is up and running.

Remember this is still the planning stage with options to change direction. Much better that it happens here before a commitment is made to families, young people, children or those committed to working with them.

DEVELOPMENT ▶   Formulation ▶   Identification ▶   Clarification ▶

Development of aims and objectives

Remembering that aims and objectives need to be clear and agreed, it is worth spending time at this stage of planning to get this right. The aims are likely to be pretty broad, reflecting long-term and overarching goals that are a recognized part of the church's overall and long-term vision. These could already be clearly defined and accepted by the church council and wider congregation. The aims will be more concerned with the 'why' rather than the 'what'. It is the job of this smaller planning group to focus on and develop the 'what'. Looking at the aims and the findings of the previous research they can set proposed objectives to serve the long-term goals of the church.

Just in case all that sounds a little confusing, look at the following example, which might help sort it out. As you may recall, one agreed Aim of St Careful's states:

> This church particularly seeks to reflect Christ's love for the young through its ministry, nurture and service to children, young people and their families.

Agreeing how they actually go about this could take a long time if left to an unspecific group of people. Let's say the earlier research has shown that there are a number of specific needs. For example:

- 11- to 15-year-olds meet outside the shops and 'cause bother'.
- Some young people come to church but don't really engage with any of the activities.
- Other young people are saying, 'We've got a bad reputation and no one lets us prove them wrong.'

With this information the planning group may be able to propose some objectives, such as:

1. To build links with young people aged 11 to 15 who currently do not access existing services and explore with them what recreational and social facilities would be of benefit to them.

2. To provide, within the church, an age-specific study group for those young people on the fringe of the church to help explore a personal Christian faith.

3. To employ a worker to work in partnership with other agencies to set up a young persons' volunteering scheme.

Objectives help clarify both the action, and the end result. Wherever possible they should be SMART.

SMART objectives

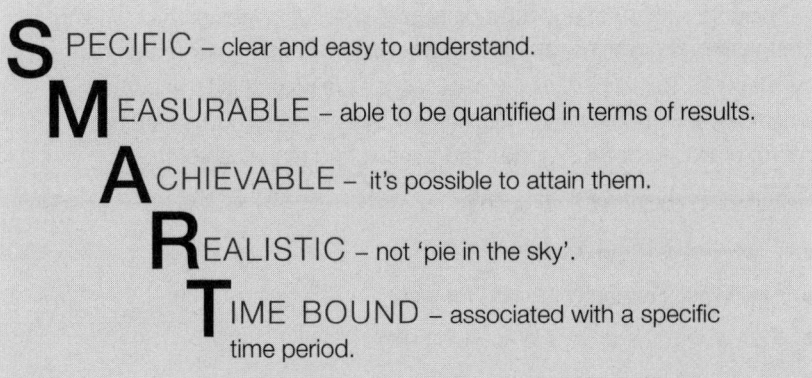

S PECIFIC – clear and easy to understand.

M EASURABLE – able to be quantified in terms of results.

A CHIEVABLE – it's possible to attain them.

R EALISTIC – not 'pie in the sky'.

T IME BOUND – associated with a specific time period.

Consider the following examples:

> 'St Careful's will do its best to help young people be of more service in the community.' This is not **SMART**.

> 'St Careful's will employ a worker in the next year, to develop a volunteering scheme for young people.' This fits the bill in all sections.

Objectives help clarify the ends to be achieved. Further strategies or plans will almost certainly be required to make them happen.

The next stage is formulation.

Development → **FORMULATION** → Identification → Clarification

Formulation of accountability and decision-making powers

It is important that there is clarity regarding responsibility and accountability. The planning group should draw up a simple document clearly proposing who should be responsible for what and to whom, and how this is to be monitored. This can save much misunderstanding, makes decision making easier, and also promotes safe practice.

If you are to receive financial support from outside funders, work in partnership with other agencies or receive charitable status, the planning group will need to formulate a more thorough governing document or constitution. This is particularly necessary if the project is to become an employer in its own right. Outside advisers can help considerably in providing appropriate models, so consult and make use of them.

A governing document will define:

* who makes the decisions;
* who has responsibility and for what;
* to whom the project is accountable;
* who will handle the money and resources.

Producing governing documents can be very time-consuming and many groups find it hard work. While the document should have provision for later change, it will save much time if you get it right for your project in the first place. So this is one of those occasions to call in help and advice. Through your research stage you should know who is available from the diocese or another denominational body, Council for Voluntary Service or some other helping agency to assist with this task.

Identification of workers and management

The planning group will identify who is needed to do the work. This may be one or a combination of the following:

- a paid full-time worker;
- one or two part-time workers;
- a number of sessional workers;
- volunteers either to carry out the work themselves or to work alongside a paid employee.

Chapter 5 will help you explore the skills and gifts paid and unpaid workers might bring.

The group will also identify which key resources are already available and which ones are needed from elsewhere. Chapter 6 tackles this very issue.

The group will identify whether having independent charitable status would be of greater benefit. There may be relevant specific legal requirements that should be understood and taken into account. Again, there are usually people available to help with such work.

The group will need to identify who is best placed to manage such a piece of work. This is crucial, as badly managed paid or unpaid work, apart from being less productive, can result in the abuse of workers and those they are working with. A piece of work well managed, by people with the time, expertise and a heart for the work will benefit those carrying out the work and those they are serving. These issues are explained more fully in later chapters.

Clarification of tasks

The planning group will begin to get a clearer view of what further tasks are required, the skills needed to fulfil the tasks, and the resources and support necessary in managing the work. With the information from the research stage and the formulated plans, they should be in a position to make clear recommendations and proposals for the next step. If a substantial piece of new work is to be embarked upon, particularly if a worker or workers are to be employed, proposals may be required in specific regard to the formation of a project management group.

There is certainly an advantage if at least some of the original planning group are willing initially to become part of a future management group. This helps with continuity and embedding the vision. It might be that you wish the entire management group to be from the church, and it is indeed important that the church is represented on the group if the work is to remain in the centre of its ministry. However, there will be others in the area who may already have involvement with children, young people or families, who can bring their expertise and may value being involved in the management of your project. The planning group would not necessarily recruit the management group but they could make useful recommendations regarding the skills and support required. Developments, thoughts, new findings and proposals will all need feeding back clearly to the church council and possibly later presenting to the wider congregation.

Take a look at what happened when St Careful used the
process outlined above . . .

Assessing need: research

Having discussed their preliminary research and suggestions,
St Careful's PCC appointed one church warden and two other
members to form the basis of a planning group. The church
council was particularly keen to see the development of work
and ministry with the young teenagers in the village, some of
whom had particularly expressed a desire to meet as a group.

Before the first meeting it was agreed to invite one of the parents
who had been active in the research to join the group. In addition,
the Methodist church in the village had shown a strong interest in
supporting a joint project with this age group, and one of their
church stewards was willing to contribute to the planning.

At the first meeting much time was given to looking again at the
views of young people as expressed in the Questionnaires. Some
of the suggestions and comments seemed outlandish, but others
weren't beyond the realms of possibility, such as:

- a warm place to hang out with some activities like computer
  games;
- a place to play our music;
- someone who we can talk to and who understands what
  we want.

Research presently ruled out the church hall, but the village hall
could be suitable and was rarely used on a Tuesday night.

Development of aims and objectives

While the churches had recognized the need to serve and minister
to this particular age group, the planning group set about
constructing some clearer aims, and later objectives, that they felt
both the churches would be willing to consider and support.

It was decided to start an early evening weekly session in the
village hall for young people in school years 8–10. The project
would offer a well-staffed safe place to meet and some

recreational and other community-oriented activities. This would be a 'pilot project' (one year) during which an assessment would be made regarding a longer-term project.

Getting to this stage took longer than expected, as the group weren't sure of the suitability of the village hall and informal 'feasibility' discussions had to take place with the chair of the village hall committee. The group soon found it necessary to record notes and action points to keep abreast of progress.

Formulation

The planning group met with the diocesan youth work adviser and sorted out a draft document outlining how funding for the project would be handled (through the church council) during the pilot stage. A small 'interim' management committee made up of church council members and two parents would act as a sub-committee of the church council, overseeing the management and development of the project.

Identification

It was recognized that at least three staff, who could be volunteers, would be required for each session. As this was a first in the village for many years, it was felt important that initial training should be required before opening, and then regular follow-up sessions of training and development for those involved. The diocesan youth work adviser and a member of the County Scouts HQ were willing to help deliver this between them. The secondment of a youth worker from the local authority was explored but wasn't available at this time.

Clarification

The Methodist church steward had previous experience of managing staff and was willing to take on the specific role of volunteer manager. The planning group also drew up a draft budget, identifying how the work could be financed through the churches, fundraising, member subscriptions and a number of small grants. A timetable of development was drafted, which included meetings with the church councils and a consultation meeting with the young people. Volunteer job descriptions were considered and informal discussions took place with potential volunteers. Finally, the planning group arranged an open meeting to which members of the two church councils and anyone else with an interest in the project were invited, to consider the plans and measure support.

Learn from the experience of Busy Street Baptist Church and their three years of Easter holiday activities . . .

Year one

No shortage of demand for holiday activities for the 8- to 11-year-olds. Plenty of willing volunteers to do a two-week play scheme, or at least there were when it was first mentioned! Unfortunately, when it came to it, there was only enough help to run for two days a week. Fortunately it *was* only two days, as they ran out of materials half-way through the first afternoon. Sessions were oversubscribed and there weren't enough alternative activities planned to keep everyone safely occupied and happy. Those involved were left feeling stressed, disappointed and thoroughly worn out.

Year two

This year, a firm commitment from volunteers was sought early on and a rota worked out to ensure adequate cover for all ten days. Unfortunately, while they were prepared to give up days during the holidays, the volunteers had little time to meet and prepare the programme together. Left to Mrs Cavalry (always keen to save the day), a programme of activities was produced, which filled the time nicely. The daily demands of being faced with creative and challenging tasks without time to prepare did not help the volunteers to feel confident. Additionally, some of the previously willing volunteers took exception to clearing up after the donkey during the Palm Sunday project!

Year three

After the challenges of the previous years all concerned decided that if they were going to try again they needed someone who could:

- coordinate and support the volunteers;
- prepare and oversee the programme;
- gather the resources that might be necessary.

As no one volunteer was available to do this, the commitment was made to employ someone for the job. Year three went so well, they are now thinking about the summer holidays!

To think about . . .

- How do we make proper use of the findings of the research?
- Has the church clear aims and SMART objectives for the development of work with families, young people and/or children?
- How do we take full advantage of outside advice?
- What will the church council need, in order to be sufficiently aware and supportive of this development process?
- How can we ensure the whole church continues to be engaged in the development of the work?

5 Who does the work?

Exploring qualities brought to the work by paid workers and volunteers, the relationship between the two, and what the planning group will need to consider in each case

The particular benefits a paid worker brings

A paid worker is in a position to develop particular skills and offer specific expertise, which benefits all involved in the work.

A paid worker can help take the strain from volunteers

The saying goes, 'if you want something doing, ask a busy person', the implication being that they willingly get involved and appear to be organized enough to fit everything in. Most congregations could identify those in their midst who would fit this description. It's often easier to approach them first rather than try to cajole those who are quieter and less forthcoming. Another common problem is that people volunteer for an hour on a Friday night and then discover the task is taking twice as long because of planning meetings, paperwork, communication and safe practice issues. The advantage of having a paid worker to take some of this strain is that it allows the volunteers some space to develop their gifts and work with the elements of the job that particularly keep them interested.

A paid worker can offer greater availability and flexibility

Another bonus of employing a worker is that of availability. Their timetable can be geared around the needs of the developing work. If that is with young people they may need to link with schools and agencies only available during the day time, when the volunteers may have their own jobs and family life to consider. An employed children's worker can arrange their own summer holidays outside of the school breaks to allow for a full programme of activities during school holidays. This may not be so easy for volunteers, if this is their only chance of getting away with their own family. Paid workers have time and greater flexibility to respond to opportunities for face-to-face work and do the necessary liaison with other agencies.

A paid worker can offer reflection and evaluation

Thankfully, there are volunteers in the church who have a strong desire and motivation to serve other people. They can be enthusiastic, willing to spend time organizing and supervising a variety of activities. Evaluating and exploring the work is a far more disciplined process and fewer volunteers find the time to develop and exercise these skills. The necessary amount of time for preparation, reflection and continued professional and personal development can be built into a paid worker's job description.

Most professional workers bring with them a wide range of working experience and, increasingly these days, some form of professional training for the job. They should have the ability to evaluate needs and set appropriate goals in response. Within any community or group of people, whatever age group, there will be a whole variety of differing and individual needs. These may not be immediately apparent. Grappling with the needs requires support and direction through supervision, possibly both by the worker's manager and additionally by external non-managerial supervision. Sadly, few churches make such provision for volunteers and, even if they did, many volunteers would find difficulty in finding the time to commit to such a process.

A paid worker can develop skills in dealing with specialist needs

A paid worker is more likely to have the time and contacts to explore and understand a range of specific issues relevant to the work that they are doing. A volunteer with only a few hours to spare may, quite wisely, be reticent to commit themselves to keeping abreast of ever-changing cultures, and issues such as drugs, homelessness, racism, mental health. While a paid worker may not have experience of dealing with all these challenges, they are better placed to access the agencies and point to the right support. Inevitably, volunteer work can only skim the surface of need. The paid worker is given time, skills and resources to delve much deeper with greater lasting effect. In addition, they have the advantage of a recognized professional role both in the church and wider community. Presenting yourself at the housing

office or the local drug project as 'St Agatha's youth worker' has a bit more
effect than as someone who 'sometimes helps with the church youth club on
a Wednesday night'.

A paid worker can be an identified focal point of commitment and ministry

Employing a worker is a very clear acknowledgement of the church's distinct
commitment to a specific area of need. The appointment can help focus the
church's understanding and also help particular people identify a friendly
point of access to the church and its ministry.

A paid worker can focus on supporting and developing volunteer work

Initiating a new piece of work takes a lot of time, patience and prayerful
commitment. If the work grows, so do the opportunities and demands.
Without proper management, support and acknowledgement, or any input
into the overall vision of the work, the volunteer can very quickly feel that the
rewards do not outweigh the sacrifices. One particular role of a paid worker
may be to offer volunteers much-needed management, support and
encouragement, which might prevent them becoming despondent or
overwhelmed. However, it's not unusual for a church with thriving and
sacrificial volunteer work to appoint a paid worker, only then to find the
volunteers and those they were working with seem to evaporate overnight.

Nurturing and retaining volunteers

Managing volunteers and the work they choose to undertake is a much-
needed skill, which is yet to be fully developed in most churches. This
becomes particularly apparent when the work is to be changed or
developed.

Nurturing volunteers

A danger in promoting the status of the specialist work is that we surround
it with a professional mystique that alienates the volunteer. There are many
aspects of working with children, young people or families. For example,
stocking and running a coffee bar or tuck shop does not require a degree

or certificate, but does require commitment that can be a valuable asset to a project. Basic important tasks can become a stepping stone to further involvement at a pace that best suits the volunteer.

Given such a large constituency and growing dependence on volunteers, it is surprising how little investment the church puts into developing good volunteer management. An exciting alternative to the expense of recruiting and employing a paid worker would be to allocate the equivalent resources to the training and support of your existing volunteers. As their skills and confidence are encouraged the results could be startling.

Retaining volunteers

Volunteers often comment, 'If I didn't do it, no one else would.'

Hidden within this kind of statement can be many feelings.

- I'm the only one who sees the need.
- I'm the only one prepared to take action.
- No one realizes or values what I do.
- No one else knows what I know and could do what I do.

Even if this is not strictly true, or at least is open to debate, the feelings are no less very real.

You might think the advent of a paid worker would help bring credit to and encourage the long-suffering volunteer, who would then be pleased to share the burden and support the developing work. This is not necessarily so. Often it simply adds the further feelings:

- What I did or do is no longer good enough!
- Now that we have a paid worker, I'm not needed.

They quietly, or not so quietly, bow out, taking with them the valuable relationships that have been formed. They can feel undermined, deskilled and disregarded. The key to retaining volunteers is listening to, recognizing, valuing and sufficiently supporting the contribution each individual makes.

The critical contribution made by the volunteer

There are certain critical advantages that the volunteer contributes to the work, which should be identified and nurtured. The volunteer is more likely to have been, and remain, a part of that local community, whereas the paid worker is likely to move on and take the local experience and knowledge with them.

In her time as a member of Godly Street church, Mrs Small has been prayerfully involved in many activities as a volunteer. When her own children were babies, she helped set up crèche facilities during the morning service. She went on the rota for doing the teas at the Mums and Tots. A few years on, and although with no hands-on involvement in the young people's work, she still gave her time to fundraising for the youth club that her own children attended. She was central in the church's support of the local women's refuge and now, with a number of growing grandchildren, Mrs Small is back in the crèche on a Sunday morning, caring for children whose parents she has known since they were children.

The paid worker is naturally inclined to justify their salary with a lively, interesting, high-profile and above all 'new' programme, claiming to touch the lives of many hundreds. The volunteer has no such need. They can quietly develop significant positive ongoing relationships, albeit with fewer people and considerably less glamour. The voluntary nature of the relationship is likely to be far more valued by the recipients than 'someone who is paid to be with us'.

The visionary paid worker will develop a high regard for volunteers. If they are sharing and develop their own skills with other adults, this can strengthen the effect of a piece of work. To know that a project does not entirely depend upon the employee, is shared by others in the local community, and potentially has a life beyond the current funding, is healthy for the work, workers and future continuity of the project.

To think about . . .

- What specific skills do we need that a paid worker could bring to the development of our work?

- How will we ensure volunteers remain at the heart of our work?

- How do we make the best use of volunteers' limited availability?

- How do we manage and support our volunteers?

- What additional volunteer support would a paid worker need in order to deliver the work?

6 Resourcing the work

Identifying and examining key resources

If you have turned to this chapter first, it may be that you had expected it to be just about money and where to get it – and most of it is! However, while there is no doubt that finances are the corner pieces and outside edges of the jigsaw within which the work is held, for the picture to be successfully completed there are many more crucial pieces that need to be fitted together. These issues will be dealt with more fully in this chapter.

Money first

In many cases finances are the main focus of discussions when looking at new projects, after all, you can't employ someone without paying them. Unfortunately, it has been known for some churches to try. There occasionally seems to be an air of unreality around church finances and management in this area. There have been known cases of churches that thought they could get round tax and National Insurance issues by calling the payments to a worker 'gifts'. Others simply exclude a 'contribution' towards an employee's mortgage or rent payments from any returns to the authorities. Whatever the intention, these practices are questionable. Christ's own response to the question of taxes is that they should be paid, and the possible consequence of not doing so could be serious legal proceedings.

Where financial resources can come from

There are three basic ways of funding an employed post:

1. The money comes from within the local church budget. In other words, from the giving of the congregation; whether by means of special fundraising, bequests or by general stewardship.
2. The money comes from some external source. It is of course encouraging that such funding can sometimes be found, although it is often a big job researching trusts and writing the necessary bids.
3. The money comes from a mixture of both.

Issues relating to funding and funders

Unfortunately, money from external sources brings some common problems for churches. The first is that such funding is often not renewable. Many posts run for the duration of the secured funding and then stop. It is possible for a post to achieve a great deal within a limited timescale, especially if it is set up specifically to initiate and stabilize a project that will then run with volunteers alone. However, where the hope is to secure further funding in order to continue a post, this can become a distraction both to those managing the work and to the worker, who will understandably start to focus on finding another job way before the money runs out.

The second common difficulty is more subtle. When money comes from external sources there can be a lack of support in all the other ways that a local church appointment needs. The worker needs the encouragement, understanding, prayerful and practical support of those around them. Where there is a need to raise and give money, then the whole congregation is likely to have been involved in committing to the project and so have a keener interest in understanding the aims and purpose. It is essential, therefore, that if the post is to be funded from external sources, the research and planning stages of the process, as described in previous chapters, are not ignored, hurried or sidestepped.

Where can we find funding and who might help?

There are specialist publications and web sites to help with applications to trusts. Some of these are listed in Appendix 6 at the back of the book. Your denomination or church network may be able to help. The process of writing bids is time-consuming and offers no guarantee of a favourable outcome, but it is possible to access secular funding for posts without compromising your integrity – even when a trust's purposes specifically exclude promoting religion. The Local Authority Compact, which should guide local authorities in relating to community groups, specifically states that they should not exclude organizations from funding simply because their overall main purpose is religious worship. The decision should be made on the basis of the criteria as they apply to a specific project or post.

What should the salary be?

This naturally depends on the nature of the post, the qualifications and experience you hope to find, and on what your budget is. It can be very helpful though to use some kind of comparative process and it might be useful to look at

- JNC pay scales. These are nationally negotiated and used for most posts in local authority youth and community work. They are a helpful reference point when fixing salaries. The scales are published along with detailed descriptions of the kinds of responsibilities that attach to various points on the scale. For full information see the CYWU web site (www.cywu.org.uk/index.shtml). This scale is the one most commonly used by local authorities and they should also be able to supply any further information you might need.

- Stipend rates. Or for independent congregations, what you pay your minister, taking into consideration not just the basic rate of pay but the added costs of housing in your particular area.

Setting the pay within an established and stated national scale also offers reassurance to potential candidates that there is a recognized progression, and the salary is not static.

What to budget for

Paying the salary is just the start. It is also essential to consider:

- Employment costs. Salary, National Insurance, pension, supervision costs.

- Housing/housing allowances. A tent in the church yard won't do!

- Travel and subsistence. How's the worker going to get to that meeting on the other side of town?

- Training resources and materials. Covering the costs of the worker's training and any that they might provide to volunteers, for example.

- Insurance. For the worker, the work, the buildings and equipment and perhaps the management committee.

- Office facilities. Or an allowance for working from home.

- Administration costs. Stationery, telephone, bank charges, payroll, for example.

- Computer and IT costs. Hardware, software and broadband.

- Equipment purchases. You can't start a five-a-side football team without a football!

- Recruitment costs. Advertising, printing, travel expenses, hospitality.

- Miscellaneous. Having something in the kitty for the unexpected – every treasurer's favourite.

And don't forget to budget for inflation and growth. Even if the work is exactly the same year to year, the cost of it is bound to go upwards. If the work is to develop and grow, provision should be made to ensure this is properly resourced. Proper budgeting reassures those providing the funds, enables the workers to understand the limits and possibilities, and provides a guide that helps inform review and future development.

Now for the other resources

Just as you wouldn't employ someone until you knew the money was available to sustain the position, it is also essential to consider whether the other resources are in place too. It is important to consider where the worker is going to live in relation to the work that needs doing. Will the church need to help in locating and providing suitable accommodation?

The planning group will need to consider the facilities in terms of appropriate venues – your research should have identified suitable and available facilities. Take into account who might help the worker do the work, no man or woman should be an island. Finally, appoint the management group way in advance of an appointment being made so that they can develop the necessary policies and procedures ready for day one of work.

To think about . . .

- How much is this job worth?
- Who could help produce a realistic budget?
- As well as the church, who would have an interest in funding the work?
- How much money would the church locally, and perhaps regionally, be prepared to invest in the work?
- Apart from money, what other key resources are needed?

7 What do we want a worker to do?

The importance of clarifying the task and timescale

This is of course the key question in the process on which you are engaged: from deciding whether employing someone is right for you, through the recruitment, if you go that way, into the management and appraisal of a worker and, eventually, into your assessment of what has been achieved and whether the post should continue.

The chief tool in this will be the job description. It is impossible to know whether employing someone is the answer until this question has been properly explored. It is not uncommon in church life for it to be clear that there is a shortfall in an area. It may even be clear that there is plenty of work for someone to do in that area. But that is not the same as identifying that there is a coherent, doable job that you've a reasonable chance of finding someone with the right mix of skills and experience to do. Be open to the possibility that you may identify more than one job. If so, you may be more effective in offering part-time posts, or a job share.

A possible process might be:

1. Identifying the tasks. Using the results of the Research Stage list all of the tasks that are not currently being done, that you would like to begin to address.

2. Identifying, for each of them, the possible ways of getting them done. At this stage you may already see either that there are a substantial number which do not seem feasible without employing someone, or you may start to see ways of deploying the gifts and skills already available to you.

3. Grouping them together according to what they may have in common. You may find you have a set of administrative tasks, a set of training tasks, a set of planning tasks, a set of delivery tasks. These may or may not be age specific.

4. Grouping them by scheduling. If four of them must be done between 10 and 11.30 on a Sunday morning, employing one person won't help much!

5. Thinking about time more generally. It may be hard to estimate, but the better idea you have of the quantity of work to be done, the more likely you are to draw up a workable job description. This should not be taken as ruling out making an appointment with a view to developing new and as-yet-unseen initiatives, but there is no point appointing someone to dream dreams, start new initiatives, develop emerging children's work, if 40 hours' work a week already exists that the worker is expected to maintain. Worse still, 40 hours of work not in the job description, but just waiting to be dropped on someone once they arrive.

Sometimes it is possible, and can be helpful, to set a target that safeguards one aspect of the work, for example, at least 15 hours will involve face-to-face work with children. Do remember that every effective hour spent face-to-face with children, young people and families requires sufficient time to plan, prepare, record, follow up. Time also has to be allowed to receive regular supervision sessions and possibly to offer support to volunteers. Receiving regular supervision and offering structured support to volunteers are vital. Adequate time must be allocated from the outset.

Developing a job description

A good job description serves several purposes. It will:

- clarify what the employer's expectations are;
- set realistic and achievable targets for the work;
- provide a framework for the work, which identifies boundaries and opportunities;
- provide safeguards for the worker and the employer;
- describe the relationship between employee and employer;
- outline the roles and responsibilities;
- set out the key terms and conditions of the employment; for example, salary, hours, annual leave entitlement, etc.;
- state clearly a process of review;
- point to the other policies and procedures relevant to the project.

This is not about building a wall for people to climb over, it is a vision that you want to be able to share and achieve together. So, at this early stage the praying, the listening and the talking have to be done. As the potential employers, you must know clearly what you want. While the job description needs to be clear about what you initially want to see achieved, there also needs to be sufficient flexibility and breadth to allow organic growth once the worker is in post. It will therefore need to be reviewed at regular intervals. Once in post, a worker's terms and conditions and their job description cannot be legally changed without their consent. All the more reason to establish an environment of open consultation and shared development from the outset.

Timescales

If the vision is clear, it should be possible at least to sketch an outline development time plan, possibly broken down into six-month periods. Inevitably, the further you plan ahead, the sketchier the plan will be. You will need to build in the provision for acting on the findings of review after each period. This document can be helpful to the church and other funders in understanding the nature of the work and some of the expected positive outcomes.

Next steps

If by now, the planning group and the church, and any other funders, have concluded that an appointment is the right next step to take, you are into the recruitment process, and we are into a new chapter.

To think about . . .

- Have we considered different ways of achieving the task?
- Is the task doable in terms of the resources and support available?
- What is a reasonable timescale, considering the nature of the task?
- Has enough work been done on clarifying and presenting the task to others?
- Is there sufficient focus and clarity of task upon which a job description can now be based?

Part Three

Appointment procedures

8   Job descriptions and contracts

Exploring further the 'whys' and offering some guidance on the 'hows'

Deliberate omissions

This book purposely does not contain sample job descriptions or contracts of employment for very particular reasons:

- Employment law and good practice are continually developing and therefore it makes most sense simply to point readers to sources of up-to-date information. Some of these sources are listed at the back of the book in Appendix 6.

- While we wouldn't suggest that a church or project should try to write such documents without a reasonable template, there are dangers of restricting the work and its development by carelessly copying the work of others.

- Job descriptions and contracts of employment are legal documents that churches should always seek specialist guidance in producing.

The job description

Your research and planning will have enabled you to develop an embryonic job description. The finished item is a necessary tool, firstly in the recruitment process, and then in the continuing management and direction of the work. A job description is a brief, yet clear and complete picture of the purpose and functions of the job you want the worker to do. As far as possible it should remove any potential uncertainty concerning the post. Once someone is appointed, it should be reviewed each year at an appraisal meeting, so that it continues to be accurate. Diocesan, Church Network or other advisers welcome consultation about such matters. This is a particularly good time to use them and their expertise may well make this process easier and less daunting.

The job description should include:

- job title;
- to whom the worker is responsible;
- required tasks of the job;
- length of employment;
- skills and qualifications needed;
- work base;
- whether it is a full-time or part-time position (giving a pro rata percentage for part-time contracts);
- days/hours and arrangements for time off and time in lieu (this can be tricky to define, but the clearer the better);
- salary and other financial arrangements.

Person specification

For recruitment purposes a person specification then needs to be prepared, which details the characteristics and abilities required in the person you are seeking to appoint. This should be developed from the job description itself, rather than from preconceived ideas of the sort of person who is to be appointed. So refer back to and work from the list of tasks contained in the job description.

It helps to define both the *Essentials*, describing the minimum necessary requirements for the post, and the *Desirables*, describing other aspects that would be beneficial to the worker and work. List them under the following headings:

- Qualifications. Some areas of work may require minimum standards.
- Experience. This could be defined in length, breadth or specific areas.
- Skills and abilities. These might be transferable skills from a range of careers.
- Attitudes. Try not to end up with a list of total contradictions!

NB Think carefully before determining that something is 'essential' as this could exclude someone who is potentially the best person for the job. For example, stating that a certain qualification is essential could prevent the employment of someone with years of experience equal to any formal training.

The majority of the person specification will relate to the identified tasks, but it is also wise to include matters that relate to the ethos of your project, and the values you espouse. It may be tempting to take these as read. 'We're a church. We're Christian. End of story.' But do you really not mind what flavour of churchmanship? Is denominational adherence important? It may not bear any relevance to the job or person you are seeking. But if it does, then be clear and upfront about it. If you aren't and you then use it as a selection criterion, you may be acting illegally.

There is another important legal point here. Equal Opportunities legislation only allows a church to specify that an employee must be a Christian if this is a genuine occupational requirement of the post. It is not possible simply to assert that all employees must be Christians because you are a church. There must be reasons, relating to the ethos of the organization, and the requirements of the particular job. So spell out, based on the job description and on your organization's ethos, the reasons (where they exist) for requiring a specific faith or affiliation.

The job description and person specification will be an essential part of recruitment and selection regardless of whether you are looking for a full-time or part-time worker.

What about volunteers?

A less formal person specification and job description can also aid in the recruitment of volunteers. Consider outlining the roles and responsibilities of the job, the time commitment, the support and training available and the skills and qualities you are looking for. People are often keener to commit themselves if they are clearer about what they are letting themselves in for. Something clear and simple in writing will also offer safeguards and structure for the volunteer and for the person managing them.

Contracts for paid workers

This whole section will appear daunting in parts to those unused to dealing with legal issues. But employing someone is a big step, which entails responsibilities, particularly towards the person you appoint. There is not only a legal but a moral duty to treat this person properly. A contract is a formal record of the terms and conditions on which the post outlined in the job description is offered. Once again, a reminder that it is advisable to take specialist advice. A congregation member with legal or Human Resources experience or a contact in your local authority may be a great help and willing to help with their expertise, but won't bear any legal responsibility if you are later found to have got it wrong.

All employers are legally obliged to provide employees with a written contract, within a defined period of commencing work. Any changes in a contract after that period can only be made by agreement with the worker. So don't leave it until the appointment is made to produce the contract or you may run out of time. In many cases workers ask to see the contract prior to accepting the appointment.

The contract should include:

- employer's name;
- place of work and an indication of where an employee is to work at various places;
- employee's name;
- job title;
- date employment commenced;
- date employment is to end (if for fixed period);
- scale and rates of pay and interval period between payments;
- housing arrangements where these form part of the remuneration package;
- hours of work;
- holiday and sickness entitlement;
- pension arrangements;
- period of notice required from both parties;
- grievance and disciplinary procedure;
- supervision arrangements;
- appraisal arrangements;
- length of probationary period.

Employees' handbook

Some of the policies to which the contract makes reference can be laid out separately and kept in an employee handbook. Producing an employee handbook, possibly in a loose-leaf ring binder, makes it easier to access and makes updating it more practical, particularly where the church employs more than one person. It also gives an opportunity to bring together a whole collection of important documents and policies that need to be readily available to paid and volunteer staff. A list of some of those policies is at the back of this book in Appendix 5.

Workers' rights

Parliamentary acts or regulations give an employee a number of statutory rights that apply whether expressed in the contract or not. At the time of writing these include the right:

- not to be discriminated against on grounds of sex, race, disability, marital status, sexual orientation, age or religion (for the latter see note (a) in the section below);
- to equal pay with members of the opposite sex if doing the same work or work of equal value;
- to statutory holiday leave;
- to an itemized pay statement;
- to maternity leave and the right to return to work;
- to paternity leave, parental leave and emergency family leave;
- to notice of termination of employment;
- not to have deductions from pay unless required by law or agreed by the employee;
- to redundancy pay (after two years and unless a waiver clause has been included in the contract);
- to a safe system of work;
- to hours in line with the Working Time Regulations (see note (b) in the next section);
- to statutory sick pay;

- to time off for public service or to look for work if declared redundant;
- to trade union membership;
- not to be wrongly or unfairly dismissed;
- to a written statement of the main terms of the contract.

There are also 'implied terms' accepted in law, e.g. a mutual duty of care that binds employer and employee to take reasonable steps to ensure the safety of others, an employer's right to organize and reorganize the work (but this must be done fairly and with adequate consultation) and an employer's duty not to change material terms of the contract unilaterally.

Other legal requirements

(a) There is a general legal ban on discrimination on the grounds of religion, but there are exceptions for organizations whose ethos is religious. However, as noted above, these are only for posts where there is a genuine occupational requirement to appoint, say, a Christian.

(b) The Working Time Regulations 1998 (SI 1998 No.1833) implement the European Union Working Time Directive 94/104. Introduced to ensure the health and safety of workers, they stipulate minimum rest periods and a maximum limit on working hours. The regulations apply to all employees over the minimum school-leaving age with a contract of employment. The relevant provisions for an adult employee are set out below. Should you employ someone under 18, please be aware that different provisions apply.

The Working Time Regulations

1. A worker's working time, including overtime, must not exceed an average of 48 hours in each 7 days.

2. If the worker claims this right not to exceed the 48 hours, then he or she must not suffer any detriment because of it (such as reduced chance of promotion, for instance).

3. A worker can agree, if he or she wishes, to work longer than 48 hours per week, but this agreement should be made in writing with the employer.

4. Employers are obliged to keep records of the hours worked.

5. Workers are entitled to a rest period of not less than 11 consecutive hours in each 24-hour period worked.

6. This rest period may be interrupted for certain types of work where the activities are split up over the day (or are of short duration).

7. Where a worker's daily working time is more than 6 hours, he or she is entitled to a rest break (of at least 20 minutes).

8. Workers are entitled to at least 24 hours' uninterrupted rest in each 7-day working period.

9. As an alternative the employer may choose to provide either

   (a) Two rest periods of 24 hours in each 14-day period worked, **or**

   (b) One 48-hour rest period in each 14-day period.

10. Workers are entitled to at least 4 weeks leave per year paid at the rate of a week's pay for each week of leave.

And finally . . .

Once again don't forget the volunteers. While a contract is not a legal requirement for volunteers an agreed statement of commitment can be very helpful. It will make it clear what will be expected of them and what they can expect of the church in terms of support and training. Such an agreement also recognizes the value and significance of their contribution to the work that is being undertaken.

To think about . . .

- Who will ensure we understand and provide the right contract?
- How much time will be required to get an agreed contract prepared?
- Who will draft the policies appropriate to our work?
- Would our volunteers welcome, and the work benefit from, a 'volunteer contract'?

9 Recruitment, interviews and the selection process

Attending to key elements that will contribute to fair and effective recruitment

It is imperative that you are well prepared before you get to the actual recruitment stage. The amount of work may at times seem tedious but without it you may be selling both your church and the candidates short. By not preparing and equipping yourselves adequately, you may fail to allow all candidates to demonstrate their full potential, and in the end it will be your church and your work that misses out.

Getting prepared

There are a number of things that you will need to have agreed before the interview itself, many of which should have been prepared prior to any advert being placed.

Application forms

There are a number of ways that you can invite people to apply for a position with your church. These include sending them an application form as a response to their request by phone, Internet or letter; requesting the provision of a CV, or an application letter detailing their reasons for applying for the position and what they feel they may bring to it. Generally, using the model of an application form allows you to extract more precisely the information that you require, and makes the task of shortlisting candidates fairer and quicker.

Information packs

Each applicant should receive an information pack, preferably when the application form is sent out or possibly when they are called to interview. This should at least include the job description and salary range, the vision for the position, information about the church, the general area, and any history that is relevant. It may also be good to include details of any youth/children's work going on in the area, whether church-based or statutory. The more information you offer, the easier it is for the candidate to assess for themselves their suitability for the task required. This can save you time in having to deal with inappropriate applications.

References

You should request two or three references, at least one of which must be of a professional nature. These can help confirm what the applicant has presented and also give you a variety of perspectives on the individual. Please ensure that a candidate knows *before* you contact the current employer for a reference. You are free to decide at what stage you take up references, e.g. right at the start or alternatively when you have decided which candidate you would wish to appoint. A referee is more able to give a proper appraisal if they too are supplied with proper information about the job, e.g. job description and person specification, on which they can be asked to comment upon the candidate's suitability. For speed, telephoning a referee following interview can be convenient in the decision-making process, but this should still be followed up in writing before a formal written offer is made.

Advertising

To reach and attract the right candidates for the position, the advert will need to look attractive, professional and well presented. Careful time-planning will be required to meet printing and recruitment deadlines. The more places the advert is to appear, the more complicated this is – so start thinking well ahead.

Think carefully about the wording of your advert. The pool of suitable workers is not huge! It is your responsibility to ensure that your advertising of a post (both any actual adverts, and the methods you choose to use taken as a whole) is non-discriminatory. Remember, this does not mean that you cannot ask for a Christian. If you can show there is a genuine occupational requirement of an understanding of, and commitment to, the faith because of the ethos of your organization, then it is fine to say so. However, you must not exclude qualified people from applying, either in what you say or how you publicize the vacancy.

In particular, although word of mouth and targeting contacts are both useful parts of an advertising strategy, if you use only these it will almost certainly be discriminatory and could lead to legal action. A balanced approach including at least one nationally published advertisement is best. Email networks have become a cheap and quick way of broadcasting your needs. But think carefully, web site adverts are available all over the world, and your generous offer of travel expenses could attract some unwanted attention.

Although you naturally wish to attract interest, it is important to try to limit the number of unsuitable applicants by being as specific as possible about what the job involves and what your requirements are. These should be based on the job description and person specification. It is helpful to include the salary or salary range. The advert will need to say that the post is offered subject to a successful Criminal Records Bureau enhanced disclosure. Take a look at other adverts in Christian and youth work publications and you'll quickly get a measure of what is necessary. Get someone else to proofread your wording as typos can be difficult to spot.

The interview panel

Members of this panel should be drawn from a number of areas, although you should be careful to keep the total number on the panel as small as possible. Large numbers not only intimidate the candidates, but also make decision making more difficult. To enable continuity some of the panel should be drawn from any committee involved in the process to date. This will ensure that the vision is clearly communicated. In addition to this we strongly recommend that you involve someone from outside your local church, such as a church youth or children's work adviser. They will be able to offer some external perspective with specific expertise in their particular field.

The interview panel should be well briefed in both the background to the job and the situation. They should be involved in the processing of applications and the shortlisting of candidates (see below) and should be consulted at every stage of the process. A suggested remit for such a group is to be found at the back of this book in Appendix 2.

What to do if no one suitable applies for the post

Do not be too downhearted. Many churches find they need to advertise more than once.

It may be useful to ask those who made enquiries why they didn't go on to apply. You may need to review where and when the advert was published. You may also need to review the wording of the advert and the timescale given for response. If you are confident in your research, planning and advertising of the post, it may simply be that the right person or people weren't available at the time of asking.

Shortlisting

Once you have received the applications, it may well be advisable to shortlist those you ask for interview to, at most, four. The best way to achieve this is by working as an interview panel to match the skills of the applicants to those 'essential characteristics' on your person specification (see above). If you still have too many, you may like to match them to the 'desirable characteristics' on your person specification. Throughout the recruitment process, keep a written record of your reasons for accepting and rejecting candidates in case of allegations of discriminatory practice at a later stage.

It is important to let the applicants know, in writing, as soon as possible whether or not they have been shortlisted.

The interview

The next stage of the process is the interview itself. It is becoming more and more common for this to take the form of a whole day or a weekend. The additional time allows opportunity for others, including young people, to meet and express a view about candidates. However, care should be taken that it is understood by all who meet the candidates that it is the interview panel alone who will be making the final decision, and that this will be based on many factors that may not be known to most of those who meet the candidates.

Given that a new post could also result in a candidate's partner and children having to relocate, the church may wish to invite family members. However, great care should also be taken that the decision on who should be appointed to the post is based solely on the applicant, and the interview process, not on the perceived strengths and weaknesses of those to whom they happen to be attached. Overall it will help the candidates and the interview panel if someone with no part in the decision-making process is always on hand to act as friendly host or hostess for the duration of the interview process.

The interview panel should be well prepared prior to the day, knowing the agreed tone, format and content of the interview. They should all know the role that they are to play in asking and answering questions and who is going to begin the questioning process. The main questions should be open-ended (no possible yes/no answers) and aim to give equal and best opportunity for all candidates to express the experience, skills, abilities and attitudes identified in the person specification. It is important to avoid potentially discriminatory questions. For example, 'This job requires a lot of evening work. How will your partner feel about this?' may be asked with the best of intentions but may be regarded as potentially discriminatory. The same concerns may be addressed by simply rephrasing the question, for example, 'This job requires a lot of evening work. How do you feel about this?' It may be appropriate to ask candidates to prepare and present a short presentation on one aspect of the work. If so, ensure the candidates have a clear brief. Ensure they have a time limit and know what equipment will be available. Remember that presentations will require significantly more time in your overall interview timetable.

Key elements in the formal interview process

- Introduction. A chance for candidates to meet the interviewing panel, settle in and be clear about the process.

- Set-up time. If candidates are to make presentations, a few minutes to set up and make ready any equipment.

- Opening questions. Something like, 'What attracted you to apply for this post?' This helps the candidate settle in to the interview.

- Main questions. These are to enquire more about the candidate, to verify any information given beforehand (on the application form, for example) and to tease out the candidate's skills, gifts and reflection on experience. This process is also to gain an insight into the candidate's personality. You may include a description of a realistic scenario and ask the candidate to outline the issues it raises and what action they might take.

- Closing questions. These are to bring the formal process of interview to a close and possibly to ensure all factual information has been obtained.

- Candidate questions. The opportunity for the candidate to ask anything that may not have been made clear or they are particularly curious about.

- Last word. Ask the candidate whether they feel they have had sufficient opportunity to present themselves, and if there is anything else that they would wish the interview panel to be aware of or take into consideration.

- End of formal process. Thank the candidate for their time, telling them clearly when and how you will be in touch, and closing with prayer if appropriate.

Decision making and appointing

After the interviews have taken place you will need to assess the candidates, deciding those who fail to match up to the 'essential criteria' and job description and weighing up the strengths and weaknesses of those who do match them. Do remember that any decisions that you make must be based on job-related reasons. It may be wise to decide upon a second choice to allow for your first choice declining.

Should none of the candidates meet at least your essential requirements be prepared not to appoint. It may be that the post can still be offered subject to reasonable and realistic additional support or training. Simply and desperately taking 'the best of a bad lot' will not do you or the work justice. Remember that this appointment is already a big commitment, so don't make it bigger than the organization can bear. Before re-advertising it may be necessary to review whether the requirements of the post are realistic and whether the advert could be better placed to attract suitable candidates.

An informal offer can be made on the phone or in person. If the person requests thinking time, then encourage them to limit it to only a few days. Longer than that and your second choice, if you have one, may have found another job. Once they have accepted, then you will need to send them a formal offer in writing, making it clear that the offer is subject to satisfactory references and Criminal Record Bureau checks.* In this letter you should include the terms and conditions of employment for them to sign and return.

You should also write to those unsuccessful candidates as soon as possible. You are not obliged to state reasons, and could inadvertently leave yourself open to an allegation of discrimination by passing on misleading information. But do be prepared for candidates to ask why they were unsuccessful. Offering constructive feedback is a tangible sign of your commitment to encouraging and developing vocations.

To think about . . .

- What mechanisms do we need in place to oversee properly and administer the recruitment process?
- Which key people need to be involved in the appointment process?
- What is the timescale required to ensure the process runs smoothly?
- Where should we be advertising this post?

---

* It is worth noting that the system for checking a person's eligibility to work with children or vulnerable adults is likely to change in the near future, when the Independent Safeguarding Authority Vetting and Barring Scheme will be introduced. More information may be obtained from the Authority's web site (www.isa-gov.org).

Part Four

Management issues

10 Good management practice

Some common requirements
for effective management

So the foundations have been dug, the concrete has set hard and the first
layer of bricks is in place. Through wisdom, your house is on firm ground
and is less likely to be washed away at the first deluge of heavy rain. Whether
employing staff or using volunteers, a reliable and effective management
group will form the cement that holds the next storey firmly in place.

Formation of a management group

Management groups often rely on untrained volunteers for membership.
They may have little experience of the role they are being asked to fulfil.
Others, who come from a background where the tasks of management
are more familiar, often already have involvement in other major concerns
and, while they can offer much knowledge and expertise at the meetings,
may not be able to take on some of the more time-consuming roles. It is
therefore important to look closely at the skills and experience needed for
the management group and identify how any gaps might be filled and
skills developed.

The planning group should have already given thought as to the
representations, skills and insights required within the management group.
Hopefully at least some of the original planning group are willing initially to
become part of the management group as this helps with continuity and
embedding the vision. It is important that the church feels it has a direct link
with this group through ministers, church council members or elders. This will
help ensure the project or work remains centred in the church's ministry. In
addition, there will be others in the area who may already have involvement
with children, young people or families, whose expertise and experience will
be of great value to the management group in understanding some of the
working issues raised by the workers.

This group will have oversight of the aims and objectives, maintaining the progress and development of the project. It is easy for the people on the ground to become so engrossed in the successes and opportunities of the immediate work that they gradually drift away from the initial objectives.

St Excited had an unexpected response to their new project for 14- to 16-year-olds. Thirty-five 11- and 12-year-olds turned up and started to come regularly. Frank, the worker, didn't like to turn anyone away and gradually changed the programme to better reflect the needs of the younger age group. Naturally the 14- to 16-year-olds stayed well away.

The responsibilities of the management group
Funding
The management group will have a rolling programme of needs to attend to. They will have to keep one step ahead of funding and resources. The workers have an important input into funding applications but the managers have the responsibility of identifying funders, representing the work to them, and completing the necessary paperwork in the required timescale. The project will come to a premature end if it runs out of money.

Policies and procedures
It is the managers who must ensure that the necessary policies and procedures for their workers to adhere to are in place. They are the ones who are going to have to attend court when an irate parent sues because an unfortunate accident happened during the trip to the seaside and the project later discovered it wasn't sufficiently insured. Make use of the Policies and procedures checklist in Appendix 5 of this book.

Communications and support
For the work to develop and gain support it needs to be publicized and communicated effectively and positively. Future funding may require

reflections and feedback from the local community and other agencies in the local area; therefore, it is helpful if good links have been maintained. Your worker may not have time to do this sufficiently and keep up with everything else they've got to do. The management group has a key role to play in this element of the work.

These are just a few things that the group will have to attend to. There are many others. Ensuring all these concerns are addressed may sound a bit daunting but there is a wealth of straightforward material and information readily available and plenty of advice already on hand to help in setting up the management group. Some useful sources of help are identified in Appendix 6 at the back of this book. Once you start looking, no doubt you'll find others.

Line management and ongoing supervision

While the management group will have general oversight, the worker and work will require a specific manager and supervisor with whom the worker meets regularly. One area of particular common concern, which church workers very often cite as causing most frustration and tensions, is insufficient local support and supervision.

For a worker to function well, it is important that there is readily available management and supervision, not just in work performance, but in pastoral overview and support. Part of a paid worker's contract of employment will outline the structure for management and supervision. This is particularly important in a church post where the lines of accountability can be confused by the number of people who have a stake, and therefore believe themselves to have a say, in the running of the project. Different models work to varying degrees of success. The required structure seems to depend significantly on the size of the church, number of staff, and nature and extent of the work.

St Tumble's first employed a part-time family worker, chiefly to coordinate the work of the weekly play group and extend the links with young parents. John, the vicar, met Christine, the worker, for an hour each month, to review progress, share information and plan ahead.

This is one model, which can work well when there is one very specific piece of work, an individual worker, and one person to whom they are clearly answerable for planning and support. However,

---

The church council agreed to extend the work to include the organization of a luncheon club and after-school group, making the post full-time, supported by a large team of volunteers.

The extension and demands of the work required much more time to be devoted to worker supervision. A bigger team inevitably brings organizational issues and conflicts of ideas and personalities, and so on. This may therefore necessitate the appointment of someone with the time and skills to give to more regular and structured supervision.

There is a distinction to be made between line management and supervision.

- **Line management** is to make sure the needs of the organization are met by the worker. The manager will be particularly concerned with the delivery of work – who is doing it, what, when and where. It is the responsibility of the manager to make sure it happens.

- **Supervision** is concerned chiefly with the quality of work – how it's being done and how it may be improved. It is the arena for the worker to explore issues and access support and is chiefly the worker's responsibility.

The two are obviously intrinsically linked. A shortage of available managers and a desire to hold fewer meetings often dictates that the two tasks are combined. This is fine if it works, that is, if both elements are available to the management and worker. The responsibility must lie with both parties to ensure it does.

Who?

Care has to be taken in choosing the right line manager and supervisor. You are looking for someone with the right experience or training in management. The vicar or minister may seem the obvious choice, but is not necessarily the right choice, as they may have more to offer by being one step removed.

Their pastoral support can help the worker develop spiritually without tying up personal growth with working performance. There are successful examples whereby the worker receives line management and supervision from a member of the management group, and receives additional specialist supervision from outside the organization. This is generally termed as 'non-managerial supervision'. It has particular benefits to the worker's development, offering a 'safe space' to explore work concerns and ideas and develop a clearer picture of what they are personally seeking to achieve through their work.

It is important for there to be a framework and discipline of meeting, which needs to be agreed and honoured from the outset. Occasional 'grabbed half hours' have only a negative effect and undermine both the concerns of the organization and the worker. Also, a distinction must be made between a staff meeting and supervision.

When?
A staff meeting may be with one or more members of staff and will be chiefly concerned with sharing information, allocating tasks and discussing the broad issues of the work. It is not generally the forum for airing individual concerns and frustrations and exploring personal development. It is essential for staff, therefore, to have a specific time set aside for individual supervision. It may be appropriate and necessary for things raised in supervision then to be brought to a staff meeting for wider discussion. Likewise, workers may need to continue in supervision matters that were first raised in a staff meeting.

Review
Another important process which aids the development of the work and the worker is the annual worker appraisal or review. This has in recent years become far more common within the voluntary sector. It offers an opportunity to record the worker's achievements and agree objectives for the coming year, so increasing the worker's job satisfaction. It is also widely recognized that this review process helps to identify obstacles to performance and identify training needs.

Many workers will agree that the preparation for a review is as useful as the meeting itself. It is easy to get so immersed in the work that its direction and value can become lost or unseen. It is essential that outcomes and expectations from the review be accurately recorded. These may need to be revisited at an agreed point, say six months on, to ensure progress. At the annual appraisal it may be timely also to review the worker's job description, ensuring it still accurately reflects the realistic expectations of the employer and matches the skills of the worker.

A safe environment

Demanding that a worker undertakes what she or he was not initially employed to do, not only has legal implications within employment law, but also engenders a climate of mistrust that will permeate throughout the project. Some churches and projects are mystified how, having lost one good worker, they have difficulty finding another. They forget that potential employees take great care to find out what has happened in the past.

Priorities can and do change. It is in everyone's interest to build a safe environment of open and honest discussion. In the meetings between supervisor and worker or managers and staff, space has to be made for proper dialogue. Using outside, and independent, facilitators very often proves fruitful. They can ask the questions others seek to avoid. They can usefully identify unacknowledged achievements and help enable differences to be dealt with in a proper context.

Volunteers

One might be forgiven for thinking this chapter only has relevance when the church takes on the role of employer. But the basic elements are just as relevant to a project entirely staffed by volunteers. There is still a need for clear lines of accountability, identified decision makers, review and supervision, which enables the workers to develop their skills with appropriate and sufficient support.

To think about . . .

- What is the extent of the management group's remit?

- What is the most appropriate structure of management and supervision?

- Who has the skills and availability to manage this piece of work?

- How are the work and worker to be reviewed?

- What management do we offer our volunteers?

11 Induction period and further development

Providing a solid foundation and framework
for the worker and the work to develop

Although the planning for, and appointing of, a worker may take up a
significant amount of time, it is important that the good work does not
stop there. To induct an employee well will help to ensure that they are
comfortable in their position and may well mean that there are fewer
problems in the long run.

Induction
First day
An initial induction should take place on the first day, with an appropriate
person or people setting time aside to guide the worker around the new
situation, answering any questions and pointing the worker to places that
they can go to for help. Time will also be required to read, understand and
discuss the policies and procedures of the project.

For many, starting the new job will also mean moving into a new home –
which may also be the place of work. This is one area where most clergy
have the benefit of experience, so even if the minister is not the worker's line
manager, she or he is a key person to involve both in planning the induction
and putting it into effect.

First weeks
The induction process is important and should not stop at this point. It
is a temptation to think that once the worker has been appointed then they
can jump in immediately, but this period is a strategic and unrepeatable
opportunity to look at the work with fresh eyes. An identified induction period
will allow the employee and manager/supervisor time to work through and
discuss policies and procedures, assess all that is going on in the situation

and the space to think strategically. It will create an opportunity for the new worker to build an understanding of how the church, area and people work, and to form important relationships. Setting aside this time for proper groundwork should result in a more strategic, rather than reactive, way of working, which can often happen if someone 'hits the ground running'.

However, it can be deeply tedious to do nothing but observe. A wise church will have identified before the arrival of a new post holder some immediate tasks for them to get stuck into. Where there was a previous post holder, these may well be the gaps that have been left: but unless you have specifically recruited a like-for-like replacement, beware of pushing a square peg into a round hole.

Further development
Shared responsibility
It is important not only that the management committee and church leadership understand this, but that the congregation also realize that the worker needs time to settle in. It is possible for appointments to flounder or be soured in the first few days or weeks of the worker taking up their position. Even if the appointment is given to someone well known from the local congregation or community, space will still be needed for both the worker and community to adjust to the new role.

Wider recognition
Both paid and volunteer workers benefit from their labours being properly recognized. This may come in the form of a title. In some churches it may also involve a public commissioning or licensing, either locally or on a regional basis. Consult and identify what the proper and appropriate form of admission to the work and/or ministry should be. This can be a good opportunity to launch and raise the profile of the church's commitment to a new area of ministry.

Maintaining and establishing networks
The worker may have already gained from being a part of a network of workers involved in similar work, locally, regionally or even nationally. Explore

with them how such a link can be effectively maintained or established. Attending regional and national conferences may help a worker deepen their understanding of the work and bring attention to new resources.

Ongoing training and development

Everyone benefits from training and so it is important that right from the start the worker is able to develop their skills. Without training, workers can lose touch with important things, such as current legislation and trends. In addition to this, to train someone in a specific area will mean that they are more effective and better equipped to do that work. This can benefit the individual, the work and the church. It is also important to make the most of the increasing number of local youth and children's work training opportunities, helping to establish evidence of a basic set of competencies that will increasingly be required by all children's and youth workers.

It is also worth remembering that if a worker is expected to train volunteers or supervise other workers, then they must be equipped for this task. Some training may take the less formal approach of constructive feedback from a supervisor or outside consultant. Make sure that the management committee together with the worker think clearly about their training and development needs right from the start. All training costs time and money, and should have already been budgeted for realistically.

Safeguarding children, young people and those who work with them

Safeguarding children and young people is the responsibility of everybody. Those managing the work have a particular role in ensuring policies are understood and applied in every aspect of the work. In the early stages of a project or post it is important to establish good practice and ensure standards are maintained by all involved in the work. The *Keeping It Safe* standards are reproduced in Appendix 4 at the back of the book. Further guidelines and training are accessible through regional churches' child protection officers and organizations such as NCVYS and the Churches Child Protection Advisory Service.

Personal development and calling

The worker will bring with them many fruits of experience and training. Others
will have supported him or her as they gained and developed the skills that
you now wish to use. So in turn, your church should show commitment to
the personal development of your worker, even if this is chiefly to the
advantage of others at a later time, and in another place.

That we are all called by God to serve him in all that we do and in all whom
we meet is pivotal to the work of most church children's, youth and family
workers. Very often they have taken a conscious decision to develop and
share their skills within and in the name of the church. As employers and
managers we have a duty of care. As the church we have the additional
privilege of sharing together in Christ's calling and ministry.

To think about . . .

- Who needs to be involved in drawing up a thorough induction
  programme?

- What initial tasks and support would enable the worker to positively
  find their feet?

- What are the initial and ongoing training needs of our worker?

- How will the congregation understand where the worker fits into
  the structure of the church?

- How best to ensure that there are opportunities for professional
  mutual support?

- How might we support the worker's personal development for
  the benefit of all?

12 Knowing how things go wrong

Identifying just how much you now know!

Unfortunately, the things that go wrong often have more effect and last longer in the memory than the many more things that went right in a project or post. With reflection and hindsight it is usually relatively easy from the comfort of the adviser's office chair to see how the situation may have been prevented.

Most preventative measures have been explored in this book. So here is a useful test of your reading skills, memory and understanding. Read through this small selection of real-life scenarios and see if you now know how the problem might have occurred and could possibly have been prevented. You may be surprised by how much you now know. Alternatively, you may feel you need to revisit some parts of the book. While names have been changed to protect those involved, the situations are no less real.

St Demanding

St Demanding employed a youth worker two years ago. Many rejoiced that eventually someone with sufficient energy was available to look after the young hearts and minds of the parish. Apart from the twice-weekly youth clubs, and developing links with local schools, the church discovered that their new worker also had musical talent and quickly involved him in creating a music group to aid Sunday worship. Of course rehearsals were needed a couple of times a week, but that was fine as the young people were so very keen. Being an athletic sort, the worker was also quickly snapped up by the school to help with the football team who went from strength to strength in the local schools league and special Challenge Cup. Unfortunately 18 months into the contract the worker went off sick with a stress-related illness.

Cap-in-Hand Community Church

Having identified the need and presented the case, the Cap-in-Hand Community Church was successful in obtaining a grant towards an after-school children's club from a major national charity. This covered three-quarters of a children's worker's salary over three years. In addition, they were able to meet the running expenses of the project from a number of smaller local trust funds. After six months the need for a Breakfast Club emerged along with a small one-off grant. It was decided to employ the excellent worker full-time in the hope that additional funding would follow. However, in order to ensure enough money was in place to pay redundancy and other administration costs the project had to close prematurely at the end of the second year, much to the frustration of the church and disappointment of local parents and children.

St Onlooker

Employed to work with families on the local housing estate, the family worker at St Onlooker soon settled in and began to build a relationship with those outside the church, as per the job description. All sorts of productive projects began, improving the life and atmosphere of the community. However, the congregation in the church failed to grow in numbers and questions were asked at the church council as to what benefits were to be gained from this worker who was costing so much money. Eventually, feeling isolated, unsupported and undervalued, the worker left, leaving the community feeling equally isolated, unsupported and undervalued.

Appendices

Appendix 1
Crucial questions checklist

These are the questions the book has set to get you thinking. You may wish to refer back to the chapters to help find an answer.

1 Laying firm foundations

- What has our church learnt from previous experience of developing work with a particular age group?

- What are our declared and undeclared reasons for focusing on this particular piece of work?

- How ready are we to face the challenges that new work will present?

- Are we committed to being patient and thorough?

- Who is prepared to take a lead in this development?

3 Stage 1: The Research

- Given our location and the nature of the work, how extensive will our research need to be?

- What period of time may we need to allocate to the research stage?

- Who might we ask to oversee the research stage?

- Are there others outside the congregation whom it would be important to include at this early stage?

- How, where, and to whom, should the research be presented?

4 Stage 2: The Planning

- How do we make proper use of the findings of the research?

- Has the church clear aims and SMART objectives for the development of work with families, young people and/or children?

- How do we take full advantage of outside advice?

- What will the church council need, in order to be sufficiently aware and supportive of this development process?

- How can we ensure the whole church continues to be engaged in the development of the work?

5 Who does the work?
- What specific skills do we need that a paid worker could bring to the development of our work?
- How will we ensure volunteers remain at the heart of our work?
- How do we make the best use of volunteers' limited availability?
- How do we manage and support our volunteers?
- What additional volunteer support would a paid worker need in order to deliver the work?

6 Resourcing the work
- How much is this job worth?
- Who could help produce a realistic budget?
- As well as the church, who would have an interest in funding the work?
- How much money would the church locally, and perhaps regionally, be prepared to invest in the work?
- Apart from money, what other key resources are needed?

7 What do we want a worker to do?
- Have we considered different ways of achieving the task?
- Is the task doable in terms of the resources and support available?
- What is a reasonable timescale, considering the nature of the task?
- Has enough work been done on clarifying and presenting the task to others?
- Is there sufficient focus and clarity of task upon which a job description can now be based?

8 Job descriptions and contracts
- Who will ensure we understand and provide the right contract?
- How much time will be required to get an agreed contract prepared?

- Who will draft the policies appropriate to our work?
- Would our volunteers welcome, and the work benefit from, a 'volunteer contract'?

9 Recruitment, interviews and the selection process

- What mechanisms do we need in place properly to oversee and administer the recruitment process?
- Which key people need to be involved in the appointment process?
- What is the timescale required to ensure the process runs smoothly?
- Where should we be advertising this post?

10 Good management practice

- What is the extent of the management group's remit?
- What is the most appropriate structure of management and supervision?
- Who has the skills and availability to manage this piece of work?
- How are the work and worker to be reviewed?
- What management do we offer our volunteers?

11 Induction period and further development

- Who needs to be involved in drawing up a thorough induction programme?
- What initial tasks and support would enable the worker positively to find their feet?
- What are the initial and ongoing training needs of our worker?
- How will the congregation understand where the worker fits into the structure of the church?
- How best to ensure that there are opportunities for professional mutual support?
- How might we support the worker's personal development for the benefit of all?

Appendix 2
Group remit suggestions

Research group
Endorsed by church council to:

- Research the local needs of children, young people and/or families.
- Consult church volunteers already engaged in associated work.
- Consult other local representatives and agencies, e.g.

  the local authority, police, schools, resident groups,
  voluntary organizations, local churches.

- Explore available resources:

  local, regional and national funding;

  potential partnerships with other churches, groups and agencies;

  buildings and equipment that is available or may be adapted.

- Assess availability of advice and ongoing support from:

  diocesan/regional church, Council for Voluntary Services,
  national charities.

- Assess implications of appointing a paid worker in terms of:

  salary/housing, working budget, recruitment, management
  and supervision, existing work.

- Present findings and recommendations to the church council.

Church council/s in further consultation with congregation/s and other interested parties to: receive research findings, agree preliminary aims and objectives, gauge commitment and agree further process of development.

Project planning group
Appointed by church council to:

- Develop a project management group that includes the necessary skills, e.g. management, finance, youth/children's work.

- Formulate a working constitution/governing document.
- Identify lines of accountability and status in charity law.
- Clarify timescale and recruitment process.
- Ensure safeguarding measures are prepared.
- Oversee budget development.
- Report back to church council.

Church council/s to discuss and endorse the work of the planning group and approve the appointment of a project management group.

Project management group

Approved by church council to:

- Oversee and ensure that the aims and objectives of the project are fulfilled.
- Identify and obtain the necessary resources.
- Develop and oversee budget.
- Oversee a thorough recruitment and selection process (see below).
- Ensure the fulfilment of legal obligations as 'Employer'.
- Ensure the effective management and supervision of paid employees and volunteers.
- Ensure policies promoting good practice and safeguarding are in place, maintained and regularly reviewed.
- Regularly communicate the progress of the project to the church council/s, congregations/s and wider community.
- Review and develop the work of the project.

Recruitment and selection group

Appointed by project management group to:

- Write application form.
- Put together job information pack.
- Set interview date.
- Write and place advertisements.

- Respond to enquiries.
- Draw up shortlist from applications.
- Invite candidates.
- Conduct interviews.
- Make selection.
- Check references.
- Notify successful and unsuccessful applicants.
- Agree start date.
- Process paperwork, including the acceptance letter subject to reference/CRB check.

Appendix 3
Sample research questionnaire
Some ideas to get you started

St Careful's and Chapel Road Methodist Church are currently looking at new ways in which together we can work with and serve young teenagers in the village.

To help us respond to what is needed and check what level of support is available, we would value the following information and any further constructive comments you would like to add. Another special survey will be distributed to young people aged 11 to 14.

Your form can be returned anonymously or, if you are willing for us to contact you further, please add your name and phone number. Please return the survey to the village shop before Sunday 23 April.

Please tick as appropriate:
1. I am a member of St Careful's Church.
2. I am a member of Chapel Road Methodist Church.
3. I live in the village.
4. If not, approx. how far away?
5. I have relatives in the village aged 11 to 14 .
6. I have some direct contact with young people in this age group.

Please answer as appropriate:

7.   Do you have any experience of working with this age group?
     If so, what?

8.   What sort of special provision do you consider the churches might
     usefully consider offering to this age group?

9.   What resources are you aware of that might be used by the churches
     in serving this age group? E.g. people, places, equipment, training,
     finance.

10.   Would you be willing to help support work with this age group, and
      if so, in what capacity?

Please use the reverse of this sheet to add any further thoughts or comments
that may be useful to the research group.

Thank you for your contribution.

Appendix 4
Paid and volunteer appointment safeguards

Your church should already have an extensive child protection policy which your organization and any paid and voluntary workers will need to refer and adhere to. In the Anglican Church this policy should be in line with the House of Bishops' child protection policy, *Protecting all God's children*.

The standards reproduced below are some specific safeguarding standards developed by the National Council for Voluntary Youth Services in their publication *Keeping it Safe*. This helpful tool kit offers youth organizations practical advice and support in developing safeguarding policies and practice. It is especially helpful with regard to making appointments and managing staff. *The Keeping it Safe* standards are linked to the NCVYS accreditation scheme for safeguarding policy and practice, called Sound Systems.

The standards identify all aspects of policy and practice that need to be addressed to ensure that the activities you provide are as safe as possible. When writing or revising your policies and procedures, it is particularly important that you pay due respect to issues of diversity and equal opportunities. This is because children and young people from minority ethnic communities, or those who are disabled, are particularly vulnerable to abuse for several different reasons, ranging from a dependency on others for primary or intimate care and difficulties in communication, to misunderstandings or misinterpretations of different cultural patterns and overt or covert racist attitudes and behaviours. Due care to diversity and equal opportunities issues will ensure that you are doing everything within your means to protect all children and young people from coming to harm.

In order to meet the standards your organization must be able to provide evidence of the following:

The *Keeping it Safe* standards

1. *Organization's policies and procedures*

1.1 There is a clear safeguarding policy statement demonstrating the organization's commitment to the overall safety of all the children and young people involved with its care.

1.2 There are clear child protection policies and procedures in place. These must take into account the needs of a diverse range of children and young people. All paid staff and volunteers must be familiar with the policy and the organization's safeguarding and child protection procedures.

1.3 There are agreed statements of appropriate behaviour, i.e. codes of conduct for staff and volunteers, and for children and young people. All levels within the organization should be involved in drawing up this document. The code of conduct for paid staff and volunteers should refer to child protection policy and procedures, which should be backed up by a disciplinary procedure if broken.

1.4 There is a procedure in place on how details of parents and carers are recorded and kept. This record should state whether the child is subject to any particular care arrangements or court orders and give guidance on how staff should deal with any conflicts between parents/carers concerning the participation of a child or young person in the activities of the organization.

1.5 A confidentiality policy is in place so that children, young people, parents, paid workers and volunteers are aware of how to act if they are giving, or have been given, confidential information. This includes a policy on how to respond to information received as a disclosure from a young person. This must also take into account Data Protection principles.

1.6 There is a diversity and equality policy and procedure that prevents discriminatory practice and upholds the rights of children and young people, as well as staff and volunteers to be treated fairly. This policy and procedure must be incorporated into all aspects of the organization's work.

1.7 There is a written complaints policy and procedure, which would allow members and users of the organization to complain about any aspects of the organization.

1.8 There should be a written policy regarding risk assessments, to ensure that all reasonable precautions are taken to prevent children and young people coming to harm while participating in any aspect of the organization's activities.

2. *Reporting concerns, suspicions and allegations*

2.1 Clear procedures are in place for reporting concerns, suspicions and allegations to key workers and outside agencies. This should include how and when the information should be reported.

2.2 There is at least one named, designated safeguarding worker who is known to all staff and volunteers in the organization and trained for this role. They are responsible for disseminating and implementing child protection procedures.

2.3 Clear procedures and support systems are in place to enable all paid staff and volunteers to report, in confidence, any suspicions concerning the conduct of others or the organization itself (whistle-blowing). Where such reports have been made in good faith, but subsequently prove to be erroneous, the staff member must not be penalized.

3. *Safe recruitment and selection*

3.1 There is an agreed recruitment procedure in place applicable to all those taking part in the recruitment process, which clearly states who has what responsibilities when recruiting paid staff and volunteers.

3.2 All potential paid staff and volunteers complete an application form which includes: address details, relevant qualifications, experience and a declaration of all criminal convictions.

3.3 All new paid staff and volunteers are asked to provide two pieces of identification, at least one of which must show their address, at least one must confirm their date of birth and at least one should be photographic identification.

3.4 At least two references are taken up for paid staff and volunteers before a post is offered. One reference should be from the last employer or an organization that has knowledge of the applicant's work or volunteering with children or young people. If the applicant has not worked with children or young people before, then they should confirm this and give an alternative referee.

3.5 All interviews being held for all paid staff and volunteers involve at least two interviewers.

3.6 All paid staff and volunteers, including trustees consent to a criminal records Criminal Records Bureau Disclosure check at the appropriate level which must be received and approved by a manager before they have any direct contact with children and young people. It should be stated in the recruitment information for the position that this is a requirement.

Note: Disclosure with capital 'D' refers to the criminal records Disclosure, disclosure with a small 'd' refers to a child/young person disclosing abuse.

4. Managing paid staff and volunteers

4.1 All paid staff and volunteers are provided with a clear job or role description, which details their responsibilities and highlights all reporting structures and procedures. This should include a requirement to act in accordance with the organization's child protection policy and procedures.

4.2 All paid staff and volunteers complete a probationary period when they start with the organization, with reviews. Reviews must have a positive outcome before appointments are confirmed.

4.3 All full-time paid staff are given at least an hour of managerial supervision a month by their line manager.

4.4 All part-time and volunteer staff are provided with individual or group supervision sessions at least every six weeks.

4.5 Disciplinary and grievance procedures are in place for all paid staff and volunteers and comply with the ACAS (Advisory, Conciliation and Arbitration Service) Code of Practice. Web site details are at the back of the book.

5.   *Providing education, training and support*

5.1   A staff development programme for the organization which is reviewed on an annual basis.

5.2   A thorough and effective induction programme is in place for all paid staff and volunteers. It includes information on all the organization's policies and procedures, including those relating to safeguarding and child protection.

5.3   An appropriate level of quality training is provided to all paid staff and volunteers on safeguarding and child protection issues.

5.4   Paid staff and volunteers undertaking specialist roles, for example recruiting or taking trips, are provided with appropriate training.

6.   *Providing safer activities and trips*

6.1   The environment and activity taking place is risk assessed and risk managed, regardless of whether it is taking place at your own centre, another centre or outdoors.

6.2   Appropriate employers' liability and public liability insurance, including any additional cover, has been taken out to ensure that all aspects of the planned activities, and all people taking part, are covered.

6.3   The activity or activities being provided are properly planned and organized. Ensuring that the activities are: age-appropriate, challenging yet safe, adequately and appropriately supervised, (taking account of staff ratio, appropriately qualified instructors).

6.4   Adequate and appropriate first aid provision is provided for young people as well as for staff and volunteers.

6.5   For planned external trips and activities, the appropriate licences and accreditation are held by leaders and your own risk assessments have been carried out.

6.6   For visits abroad and international exchanges, thorough risk assessments are done by the organization or the organizing travel agency. All safety requirements for a trip in the UK should be followed as a matter of good practice, even if less stringent standards of safety apply abroad.

6.7   Any transport provided should be checked to ensure the vehicle has valid insurance, tax, MOT, seat belts and a first aid box available, and that the driver has the correct licence and insurance.

6.8   Any access to the Internet that is provided is protected by appropriate blocking mechanisms to prevent access to inappropriate sites. It is also monitored to reduce the possibility of unsuitable people making contact with the young people in your care.

Keeping it Safe – NCVYS

Appendix 5
Policies and procedures

These are some of the policies that may need to be in place to ensure
safe and good practice. They need to be readily available to managers,
paid and volunteer workers and discussed before work commences.
Rather than start with a blank sheet, obtain policies and procedures from
other projects or advisers to adapt to the needs and working practice of
your project. Procedures will need to be agreed, understood and regularly
reviewed as the work develops.

Volunteer policy
Defining the project's expectations of volunteers and what the project offers
by means of support, management and training. There may need to be
special provision for 'young helpers'.

Health and Safety
Including security, staff ratios, first aid, food safety, hazardous substances,
and equipment checks.

Confidentiality and information sharing
How personal information will and will not be shared with other workers,
management, other agencies and members of the public.

Child protection and safeguarding adults
Ensuring the safeguarding of children, young people, vulnerable adults,
and those working with them. The church should have an overall policy
with which to comply, but further measures and procedures will probably
be necessary.

Environment
How the project manages waste.

Fire
Responsibility for fire prevention and procedures in the event of fire.

Equal Opportunities
A statement of intent and process for ensuring all are treated with equality.

Recruitment of paid workers and volunteers
Particularly necessary for projects managing a growing number of workers.

Internet use
How the internet is used by workers and clients.

Bullying
Policy that also outlines procedures in dealing with incidents of bullying.

Trips, residentials and outdoor activities
Necessary safety measures for any specialist activities.

Advice regarding working (and sleeping) hours/proper breaks.

Disciplinary procedure
Explaining the legal requirements and procedures of disciplinary action against employees.

Grievance and complaints procedures
Explaining the agreed procedure when a worker has a grievance against another worker or manager.

An additional complaints procedure may be necessary for clients and members of the public to raise issues with the project.

Accident and incident reporting
The process by which all accidents and incidents are recorded, reported, and acted upon.

Risk assessment
A procedure for assessing risk both in the project as a whole, and for individual activities and specific events.

Parental consent
How this is obtained and what parental consent is required within the project.

Drugs
How the use and effects of drugs are to be managed by workers both on and off the premises.

Personal and project property and equipment
Responsibilities regarding care, storage and security.

Reimbursement
How and when out-of-pocket expenses are to be met by management for paid workers and volunteers.

Appendix 6
Online resources

These organizations offer further help and advice.

ACAS (Advisory, Conciliation and Arbitration Service) www.acas.org.uk
Information, advice and resources for solving employment problems and improving performance.

Amaze (Association of Christian Youth and Children's Workers)
www.amaze.org.uk
Help, advice and publications on employment and management best practice.

Charity Commissioners www.charity-commission.gov.uk
Help and advice regarding becoming a registered charity.

Churches' Child Protection Advisory Service www.ccpas.co.uk
Extensive range of child protection resources offering guidance and training.

Community and Youth Workers Union www.cywu.org.uk
Joint Negotiating Committee for Youth and Community Workers (JNC) national pay scales and conditions.

Keeping Children Safe www.keepingchildrensafe.org.uk
Tool-kits and sample documents to help establish thorough child protection policies.

National Council of Voluntary Child Care Organizations www.ncvcco.org
Resources for safeguarding, workforce development, evaluation guidelines, etc.

National Council for Voluntary Youth Service www.ncvys.org.uk
Help and advice, training resources, information and publications on
qualifications, diversity, etc.

National Youth Agency www.nya.org.uk
Sample job descriptions, explanation of differing qualifications and much
else of use.

Volresource www.volresource.org.uk
Web-based organization offering useful information on anything to do with
running a voluntary organization.

Still can't find what you are looking for?
Try putting subjects and key words into your Internet search engine. There is
a lot of information freely available, but do take care to check that it is up to
date and from a credible source. And don't forget, your church's children's
work, youth work and/or families work adviser may have just what you are
looking for. Perhaps they have a web site too – have a look.

Index